CW00351571

Fat is a
Spiritual Issue

My Journey

Fat is a Spiritual Issue

My Journey

Jo Ind

MOWBRAY

Mowbray
A Cassell imprint
Villiers House, 41/47 Strand, London WC2N 5JE
387 Park Avenue South, New York, 10016–8810

© Jo Ind 1993

All rights reserved. No part of this publication may be
reproduced or transmitted in any form or by any means,
electronic or mechanical including photocopying, recording or
any information storage or retrieval system, without prior
permission in writing from the publishers.

First published 1993

British Library Cataloguing-in-Publication Data
A catalogue record for this book is available from the British Library.

Library of Congress Cataloging-in-Publication Data
Available from the Library of Congress.

ISBN 0–264–67295–X

Back cover photograph by Rachel Dean

Typeset by Colset Private Limited, Singapore
Printed and bound in Great Britain by
Biddles Ltd, Guildford and King's Lynn

Contents

For anyone who is
starting again tomorrow

Foreword

by Lavinia Byrne IBVM

This is a deeply untheoretical book. It tells the story of a journey into freedom. Freedom from what? A host of voices which enslaved the teenage Jo Ind and made her a compulsive eater, someone who hated her body and was its slave, someone for whom the Promised Land could never materialize because its true location was always misplaced, someone for whom God was both enemy and ally. A host of voices which eventually communicated the will of God with force and authority because they insisted that the Word really did become flesh and that what this means in our day and age has to be renegotiated and freshly understood. These are the voices that whisper and wait.

I first met the author in 1987. Intelligent, with mocking eyes and the most beautiful complexion, she told her story with the same kind of simplicity and directness with which it is narrated here. This is the irony of course; you would never know. Looking at someone from the outside is such a perilous activity. Their truest experience – and certainly the deepest workings of grace within them – are happening at a level which is inaccessible even to their friends.

That is why the testimony of the many voices in this book

is so important. Christian asceticism has not always been a good friend to women; women have too readily been told that they are temptresses by nature (even if the apple only had a calorie count of 40) and that their bodies must be brought into submission. Women have too readily been told that the spiritual life is a life which requires subjection and denial. Indeed the spiritual tradition which first drew the adolescent Jo Ind to the life of faith made absolute demands. Jesus was her Lord and Saviour, nothing but the best would do. Conversion had one meaning only.

And yet the voices raged at her. The bathroom mirror, the size ten jeans, the BLT sandwich, her parents' divorce, sibling rivalry, the cagoules, three-chord choruses and fear of the Christian Union, chocolate, prayer, sex, love. Each in turn invited her to inhabit her own body and her own experience; each by turns demanded discernment. This book's story is the story of that discernment, the story of how Jo listened to the voices, sometimes honestly, sometimes guiltily; sometimes with joy, sometimes with fear. The point is that she kept listening. The point is that God kept enticing her, leading her into the wilderness in order to speak to her heart. How appropriate therefore, becomes the book's refrain: 'I had to trust my guts'.

At the cattle market in St Jacob's, the Amish village in Ontario, I once heard one bowler-hatted farmer remark to another, 'The bowels of the Lord's compassion were opened upon me this morning'. I flinched and found myself looking nervously at the sky. Yet where God has no guts, how can we? That summer I met Jo and began to read her first work on this book. I admire her guts for writing it, for taking the risk that goes with self-disclosure, for striving to contribute to a more healthy, sane and life-giving view of what it is to be a Christian woman – whatever your size.

Lavinia Byrne IBVM

Introduction

This is a book that I never intended to write.

When I wrote to publishers seven years ago and suggested that a book on Christianity and women's eating disorders would be a good thing, I had no idea what I was letting myself in for. I was in my last year at university and, because of my experience as a compulsive eater, felt there needed to be some publication integrating feminist thought on the matter with spirituality. I did not necessarily intend to write it myself and I certainly had not envisaged embarking on an autobiography, but I felt there was a gap on the bookshelf that needed to be filled.

Two publishers wrote back and said: 'We agree. Get on with it', so I thought it would be interesting to give it a go. I imagined it would take eight weeks.

Two years later I was still at my typewriter. The wretched book kept changing and I kept changing. There was something about the process of writing that was dynamic. I had a clear idea of what I wanted to write but the very act of finding the words deepened my original understanding, and I came to realize that I could not know what my book was about until it had actually been written.

Then there was the issue of how much I was to write my own experiences into the text. My original idea had been to write a self-help book for teenagers which did not refer to my own story at all. But as friends read the pages they said that it needed some examples, and as I wrote in anecdotes from my experience everyone said that those were the best bits.

In the end I did what I had been resisting all along – I wrote my own journey. By 1988, three years after I started, my book was almost complete, but it was so exposing I could not face having it published, so I put it in a cupboard and hoped it would go away or at least re-emerge in a less costly form.

Fat is a Spiritual Issue is an intensely personal book. It is not an ordinary autobiography in the sense that the story does not develop chronologically. Rather, it develops conceptually. That is to say, I tell my story through themes rather than in the order in which the events occurred. Each chapter starts with a leap back in time and becomes a journey in understanding up until the point at which I stopped being a compulsive eater.

I wrote it that way for the sake of clarity, but it would be misleading to suggest the insights arose neatly one after the other. They did not. They were inter-related and the process of dealing with my compulsive eating was more like spinning a web than following a straight path.

As I write this, anorexia (where people cannot eat), compulsive eating (where people cannot stop eating) and bulimia (where people eat too much and then make themselves sick) are in the news more than they were in the days when I suffered from an eating disorder. Knowing of women – simply because it usually is women – becoming ill through their relationship with food fills me with a sense of compassion and urgency. Having come out the other side of an eating disorder I really do believe that we do not need to live hung-up about our bodies and food. People can live lives which are deeper, freer and happier than that.

Today I feel just as I did when I wrote to publishers in 1985 – that if there is anything I can do to help people be free from compulsive behaviour, then I want to do that thing, however costly. If my journey can help just one person on the road to the discovery of a more liberated self then it is a story worth telling. That is why I have chosen to tell it.

Jo Ind
15 August 1992

Acknowledgements

In a sense the whole book is an acknowledgement. It is an acknowledgement of the people without whom there would have been no story to put into words.

Some, like my sister Tessa, are so much a part of me it is impossible to assess the extent to which they have contributed to my journey. Others passed through my life fleetingly but had an influence disproportionate to the moments I spent with them, like the Franciscan friar who within minutes of our meeting thrust into my hand a copy of Jim Cotter's *Prayer at Night*. 'This is your sort of book', he said. I never saw him again.

There are many between these poles, and they include Liz, Pam, Anne, Thug, Steve, Ewan, Renee and Penny. There is also a special place for Fiona, Jane and Lisa, who even after reading this story will probably still not appreciate how they challenged my faith and changed my life.

Secondly, acknowledgements are due to the professional people who urged me to see my writing through to publication. Lavinia Byrne IBVM was instrumental in this and the Rt Rev Mark Santer, Bishop of Birmingham, provided a well-aimed nudge at the right moment.

Finally, I must acknowledge the writers who have gone before me and informed my thinking on eating disorders. They are Susie Orbach (*Fat is a Feminist Issue*), Geneen Roth (*Feeding the Hungry Heart*) and Jim Cotter (*Prayer at Night*).

In the beginning was the Word:
the Word was with God
and the Word was God.
He was with God in the beginning.
Through him all things came to be,
not one thing had its being but through him.

The Word was made flesh
he lived among us,
and we saw his glory.

St John

1

A compulsively eating body

Beep beep beep, beep beep beep, beep beep beep. 'What where am –' *Beep beep beep* '– I? Oh shush.' *Beep bee* – 'Oh. It's seven o'clock. It's Monday. There was something I was dreading about today. Oh that was it. It's high-protein week. I don't think I want to get up.'

At five foot eight inches and at seventeen years of age I weighed nine and a half stone, but the figure was rapidly going up. The summer before I had weighed only eight and a half. I had decided that I was too fat and was going to do something about it. My weight was rising in direct proportion to my efforts to diet. I got out of bed.

The bathroom mirror was steamed up. My sister had just had a bath. I automatically wiped the glass with my face-flannel and looked myself straight in the eye. 'Now look', I told the face that stared back at me, ignoring the pain in its eyes, 'you never used to be that ugly but now look at you.' My hand pinched the fat that was forming around my less definite chin line. I watched myself squeeze my newly rounded cheeks and felt my fingernails press into the flesh that covered them. Looking at myself was not enough. The fact that I was disgusting had to be confirmed by touch as well.

1

There then proceeded the morning ritual that never failed. I pressed my chin as far down into my neck as my flesh would allow and there it was – a double chin. There was certainly nothing pretty about the face now. 'Just look at you', I said. 'And your face is your good feature too. We haven't even started on your body yet. Now listen to me. The reason that you look like that is the fact that you are greedy and selfish and weak. You consume such gross quantities of food that you fully deserve to look every bit as ugly as you do. Look at yourself. There on your face for the whole world to see is the hideous truth that you are a self-indulgent person. Children know how to eat, your friends can control themselves, but you cannot.'

I paused and quickly lathered the soap over the accursed face, and smiled at the contrast between my method of washing and that of the sensuous lady on the soap advertisement. I cupped my hands, filled them with water and placed the offending article into them. My hands parted on contact and I wiped the soap away. 'But' – I stared sternly into those eyes – 'today is going to be different. And the next day and the next day. Today you are going to eat only meat, fish and eggs and nothing else. Do you hear me? And if you break your diet this time I will never forgive you. Never.'

I left the bathroom, walked into my bedroom and opened the wardrobe door without looking in the upright mirror fixed inside. My body was not privileged with the same treatment as my face. I had given up looking at that a long time ago.

Inside the wardrobe hung the morbid ghosts of my former life. I drew the hangers back one by one: size ten jeans, size twelve jeans, size twelve brown cords, cheesecloth shirt, stripy shirt, see-through sun-dress, pretty-pretty Sunday dress . . . none of these was an option for me now. Their function was to remind me each morning of who I used to be. Buy more clothes in a larger size? No. What would be the point? I would lose weight. I would lose seven pounds this week and seven pounds the next. I would wear them all again in a fortnight's time. I picked out the only item of clothing that I could wear: a baggy pinafore dress, not looking in the mirror to confirm my worst fears.

2

Today was diet day so I missed breakfast. Instead I got on my knees and came before God in prayer. God of course hated my fat. He abhorred self-indulgence. I knelt by my bed and repented of my sin. 'Father, I am sorry that yet again I have failed. I have continued to stuff food into my mouth when I have had no need of it. O Lord, please, please forgive me and give me a fresh start.'

Then I read the passage from the Bible about Jesus fasting in the wilderness and meditated on the significance this had for me on my diet. I then struggled to find a way of praising God and twenty minutes later I imagined the day I was to have and consciously tried to involve God in every part.

It was quite easy to miss breakfast. I knew I was always stronger and more determined in the mornings. I started with break at school. Everyone else would be eating chocolate or drinking cocoa from the vending machine. I would have a pint of water. 'Father, please help me to be strong in you', I prayed. 'You said that the Fruit of the Spirit was self-control: give me self-control. Lord, I acknowledge my weakness; past history has assured me of my total lack of ability to control myself. Please work inside me and be strong in me.' And so it went on. I prayed through lunchtime, I prayed through the time when I arrived home from school and I prayed through the evening. I knew no other way of equipping myself with God's power, so I just trusted myself to his care and left the house.

The cold chicken was awaiting my arrival when I came home from school. I tore the skin off, dug my fingers in and gobbled it while I was still standing up. It was hardly what I felt like eating. I had only consumed two pieces of ham and three pints of water all day. Since about eleven o'clock I had felt a vague queasiness in my stomach. I had felt quite faint and tired. I had just about managed to resist the baked potato and lamb stew at lunchtime. It had only been lack of access to food that had forced me to stay on my diet through the afternoon. The thought of a cheese sandwich with lettuce and tomato was like . . . but I must not even think about it.

Evenings are always difficult. The sun goes down, the fire goes up, the curtains are drawn to the rest of the world.

3

Evenings are a time for relaxing after a hard day, in a cosy and secure atmosphere. They are not conducive to the rigorous discipline necessary for fasting. I did some work and chewed the piece of plastic that once had been my pen top. I held my stomach as it ached for food.

Perhaps, I thought, if I watched telly I would become so absorbed in the programme I would be able to rest from thinking about my belly. There was fat chance of that. On television I saw thin girls. I saw very thin girls and they had everything they wanted. All of them were rich, successful, and admired. My feeling of hunger increased as did my desire to be slim.

I thought about that cheese sandwich. I had my feet up on the sofa, my head rested on the arm. To the unattentive observer I was contented and relaxed. Inside me was civil war. The cheese sandwich was taking on larger-than-life proportions. I prayed to God. I tried to ask his power to help me. I asked the Spirit of self-control to enable me. I thought of that cheese sandwich, the texture of the bread, the wet lettuce, the thick cheese . . . I got up and left the living room and stood at the kitchen door. Should I? Shouldn't I? I could make up for it. It would only be one day. I could start again tomorrow. But I had said that yesterday and the day before. *Click*. The door opened; someone was coming. The shame of eating deterred me more than the thought of the calories. The decision was made. I went to my bedroom.

Lying on my bed, I fantasized about that cheese sandwich. I salivated, hoping that the mere thought of my teeth going through the crumbly cheese, the moist lettuce and the fibrous bread would in some way alleviate the rumbling in my stomach. It was no good. I got up to pray. I read a psalm from the Bible and tried to focus my mind on God.

If I could glimpse his holiness then perhaps my mind would be taken off my fleshly and worldly desires. So I concentrated on how perfect and beautiful Jesus was and how ugly and obscene I was by comparison. I became aware that the cheese sandwich was consuming my consciousness in a more powerful and vibrant way than God ever did. Feeling increasingly guilty, I decided to retire to bed. It was half past eight. I was not tired but my bed was a refuge. The only place I could escape from the battle was in sleep.

I started to get undressed, pulled my dress off and then my shirt, looking with disgust at my protruding breasts and extended belly. I grimaced at the white, fleshy thighs, enhanced for extra ugliness with stretchmarks. I was loathsome to myself. The bare truth was revealed and I could bear it no more. I pulled on my dressing gown and made a run for the kitchen.

A piece of dry bread was already in my mouth while I was spreading the bread for the sandwich itself. I could not wait to wash the lettuce or the tomato. I hacked off a piece of cheese, folded the bread over it and stuffed it in, swallowing it before I could taste it. As I ate I prepared the next piece. The immediate sensation of hunger was relieved and I started to slow down. What next? What had I wanted to eat all day? Cereal. I sat down for this one with a packet of breakfast cereal, a pint of milk and a bowl of sugar. I knew from experience I would only stop eating cereal when I had run out of one of the three commodities. The milk won. I moved on to eat an apple, four chocolate biscuits and half a cake.

How I hated myself now. I had done it. I had done that very thing for which I had said I would never forgive myself – I had broken my diet. I could never complain about being fat and ugly again. It was all my own fault, my disgusting, grotesque and self-indulgent fault. I deserved every bit of unhappiness I got. So then came the time of punishment. How could I punish myself? What could I do that would make me feel worse than anything else? I started all over again, beginning with the savouries and moving back on to the sweets. I forced the food down, feeling more and more uncomfortable, until at last I decided enough was enough and I crawled into my ready-made womb – my bed.

I could not sleep. I wanted to sleep. I wanted to sleep and never, ever to wake up again. How else would I stop eating food? Every day that I lived I would have to face it. It would always be there haunting me, tempting me, luring me, and I would get fatter and fatter and fatter. I would always think about it, eat it, love it, hate it. If I could sleep now, it would still be there in the morning. I was not contemplating suicide, just wishing I was dead. I imagined a land where there was no food, a place without diets, binges or fat. If I did not have a body I would enjoy living there. That would be heaven itself.

I was a compulsive eater. Trying to control my eating was like trying to pedal from Birmingham to the Scilly Isles on an exercise bicycle. That account of my day was not exaggerated, nor was it something that happened only once. I experienced that inner turmoil and outer self-abuse almost every day from the age of sixteen to the age of twenty, from eight stone four ounces to thirteen stone.

It was four years of fasting, of high-protein diets, of fruit-only diets and calorie-controlled ones. It was four years of breaking diets, of breaking into packets of biscuits and of breaking records when I stood on the scales. It was four years of dreading going clothes shopping, never going swimming, never dancing at parties and certainly not flirting. My evaluation of my life was by one criterion alone: have I stuck to my diet today?

The problem with my eating was that I could not stop. My eating bore no relation to my hunger or my need for food. My stomach could have been saying 'Send us something down to work on' or 'Steady on out there, we're overloaded', but I would have heard neither. 'Hungry' and 'full up' had become meaningless words.

When I was a child I ate when I needed food and stopped when I was satisfied. My mother would ask if I had had enough and I would say, 'Yes thank you' or 'Could you pass the biscuits please?'. I understood my appetite even before I understood my bladder.

Going on diets meant I unlearnt this basic response to my body's messages. I stopped listening to the rumbles in my tummy and started reading the directions in the book. Eventually I was so out of touch with my hunger that I ate in one of two ways: either I ate according to the calorie counter or I ate everything in sight. This pattern became so deeply entrenched in me that the idea of eating because I was hungry was like buying perfume because I liked Winnie the Pooh. Whatever had hunger got to do with it?

Accompanying my compulsive eating was a hatred of my body. I did not, I could not, I would not look in the mirror; I was revolting, I was fat. It did not matter whether I weighed eight stone, nine stone or twelve stone two, there was only one verdict: flabby. My breasts were too large, my thighs too crêpy, my hips too wide, my bum too protruding, my skin too pale, my feet too stocky, my hands too inelegant. Yuk.

Women's magazines encouraged me to hate myself, but I did not need any assistance. I actively tried to cultivate this energy in the belief that it would lead me into slimness of life. I would deliberately give myself a double chin so I could see how ugly I looked. I would dig my fingernails into my thighs, making delicate, moon-shaped bruises. Sometimes I would imagine having a knife and slicing into my flesh and hoping it hurt. Eating was not my only form of self-abuse.

I imagined as a compulsive eater that sexual relationships were not for me, or at least not until I was thinner. In the meantime I was the frumpy, anonymous blob serving drinks while slim people got together and played flirty games. Whenever I did receive the nod, the wink and 'Can I buy you another?', it was because I had been so entertaining he had not noticed my body. If I was sexually involved with people I knew and loved, it was because they were good friends – they must have been.

I knew I could not compete when it came to the real stuff. The real stuff happened in the cattle market of the pubs and clubs. I wanted to be a prize cow, I wanted to rub a high-heeled foot slowly against a silky, shaven calf, directing the eye beyond the slit up the back of my tight, leather miniskirt. I wanted medallion man to stare coolly, knock back his pint and tell his mate what he would like to do with me. I did not want to be done to, but I wanted to be sexual. As it was I sat in the corner, fat.

I would have preferred some more exotic sins to the loaf-of-Mother's-Pride variety, but as a compulsive eater I was paralysed with guilt. I was crippled with a sense of failure, of not having made it, of shame. Having triple helpings and developing a triple-fold belly was humiliating. It lacked the seedy glamour of being addicted to alcohol or drugs. It seemed excusable to be desperate or disillusioned but not to be just plain greedy.

My guilt was compounded by the fact that I was a praying person. Had I been the type who rolled out of bed each morning, brushing the sleep out of her eyes on the way to school, it would have been less of a problem. As it was I would spend an anguished ten minutes asking God to forgive me, which became a meditation on how weak and sinful I was. Sunday by Sunday I said the confession:

Almighty God, our heavenly Father *(Funny that, men don't seem to have this problem, especially not people's fathers.)*
We have sinned against you *(I have abused the body you gave me by making it overweight.)*
And against our fellow men *(It is selfish to be fat because other people have to look at me.)*
In thought *(I fantasize about food. Those baked potatoes with gooey cheese inside, sprinkled with black pepper and topped with . . .)*
In word *(I lied. I told my friends I had not broken my diet.)*
And deed *(Guess what? Same again. Sorry to bore you.)*
In the evil we have done *(See above.)*
And the good we have not done *(Lose weight.)*
Through ignorance *(No, Lord, not through ignorance. Oh would that my sins were through ignorance.)*
Through weakness *(It was Mary's birthday and that cake . . .)*
Through our own deliberate fault *(That's more like it, less of this wimpy-nimpy weakness nonsense.)*
We are truly sorry *(O God, can you hear how sorry I am?)*

8

And repent of all our sins *(I repent so much.)*
For the sake of your son Jesus Christ, who died for us
*(Help me to say with every bite that I take that it is one
more wound in the body of Jesus.)*
Forgive us all that is past *(But God I said this last Sunday
and the Sunday before and every single Sunday for four
years. How long can you go on forgiving the same old
sin?)*
And grant that we may serve you in newness of life
*(Please, please help me. Help me not to break my diet,
Lord. I'm starting on Monday with a boiled-egg-and-
grapefruit one.)*
For the glory of your name *(I would be a much better
witness if I were slim.)*
Amen *(Gosh, he's rather nice in the pew in front. Oh no,
I've started already. God, can you forgive that last sin
too, while you're dealing with the others. Help me not to
think about men every time I say 'Amen'.)*

The priest might have stood at the front and said,
'Almighty God, who forgives all who truly repent . . .', but I
did not feel forgiven. The very word 'truly' seemed to con-
demn, casting doubt on the validity of my confession. There
was a part of me that wondered if the unforgivable sin was that
of breaking your diet for the one thousand, seven hundred and
twenty-fifth time.

Being a compulsive eater meant being obsessed with figures and food. It was rare for the grey matter not to be musing
on some body matter. It was normal to be thinking of figures
all the time. Everything that I saw in the world, I saw through
fat and thin.

'The sun is shining' meant 'too fat to wear a bikini'. 'Shall
we go to the cinema?' was a question of ice creams in the
interval. A month measured the possibility of losing a stone in
weight. 'Eve ate the apple of the tree of knowledge' was about
consuming 40 calories. Even cuddling a boyfriend became 'He
can feel my fat. I hope he's not feeling my fat.' An everyday
task like buying stamps in the post office was 'She's got a nice

figure. I must look like her in a month's time. God, she's fat. I hope
I don't look like her. That means everybody in the queue must be
looking at me and thinking, "I'm glad I don't look like her. She's
fat." '

I was a compulsive eater but it was a long time before I learnt
to describe myself in that way. I could not own my problem. For
years I thought my difficulty was simply being overweight. It
was easier to say that I had a weight problem than that I had an
eating disorder. I saw my dilemma in terms of my outsides rather
than my insides: if only I had small breasts, narrow hips and neat
buttocks everything else in my life would fall into place.

Because I thought my only problem was being fat, the solution, so it seemed, was to diet. Yet the one thing in life that I could
not seem to do was to lose four pounds/half a stone/one stone/
three stone. I was determined to succeed.

That is why I was a compulsive eater for four years – I had
misinterpreted the situation. In fact my difficulty was not that I
was fat. That was merely a symptom of much deeper problems,
and while I tried to change the effect rather than confront the
cause, I never got any better. Having a different body would not
help me to eat properly. I needed to stop dieting and look at why I
had become a compulsive eater. I had to listen to what was going
on inside me.

I discovered I could not eat properly because I hated my
body. I could not eat properly because I no longer recognized
hunger. I could not eat properly because I was suppressing my
sexuality. I could not eat properly because I was consumed with
guilt. I could not eat properly because I was obsessed with food.
Because I could not eat properly I was becoming fat.

This is my story. It is the story of how I went from being a
compulsive eater to being free from the bondage of food. It traces
a journey, a journey from not admitting I had a problem to
acknowledging it, from hating my body to loving it, from suppressing my sexuality to saying 'yes' to lovemaking, from being
out of touch with my appetite to eating when I was hungry, from
being obsessed with fat and thin to being more fully alive. The
journey was one in which at least two stone just dropped by the
wayside.

The journey was all of this and more because I also had a faith. Since the age of eleven I had spent time each day meditating on a being I believed to be God. Of course nobody knows whether God actually exists or not, but I do know that as a praying person the way I imagined God affected the way I saw myself, the world and my eating disorder.

If we picture God as macho it is hard to accept being a woman. If we picture God as pure spirit it is hard to be glad to be a body. If we picture God as the paradigm of self-control it is hard to come to terms with an inability to stop eating. I prayed to a being I believed was Lord, King, Father, Son and Spirit, strong and mighty in battle, defender, fortress and judge. None of this was very helpful as I struggled with chocolate cake, swelling breasts, and being sexual, compulsive and feminine.

In fact it was not just unhelpful but actually impossible. I could not become a free human being while I continued to think of God as Rambo. As a praying person the way I pictured God was so much a part of who I was that I could not change without also developing my understanding of God. Getting to the root of my eating disorder demanded a radical reappraisal of my faith.

So, intricately woven into my story of becoming free from food is the story of my growing awareness of who God is. At one level I was losing weight, at another I was gaining insight. I was growing more deeply in touch with the one who had given me life, and changing, from my innermost being to the fat at the top of my thighs.

11

2

Body growing up and out

Unlike many people I had a womb-mate. Dominic started this curious business of living before me and took his place in the womb. I was conceived later and so had to fit in with him. I do not remember anything about it but the nurturing wall around us said we enjoyed her as a football.

My twin had got in first, according to family myth, and had hogged the best pitch, so he wanted to emerge before I was ready. I was the only obstacle between him and daylight, so he took it upon himself to push me out. That is how one dark November night we made our bawling, bald-headed entrances to the world beyond our mother.

Things were to continue as they had begun. We would share the job of feeding, one leg, one arm, and one breast each. I would put in all the cheek-work and get the milk flowing while Dominic lay back and gurgled. Once supper was dribbling out in ample abundance he would start his greedy sucking while I had to take a rest, exhausted by the effort.

My feminism runs deep.

As children my brother and I were incapable of being together without a fight erupting. It did not matter how the play or the conversation had started, the scenario was always the same: he would hit me and I would scream. My parents intervened. My father would say it did not matter what had happened, I should not scream, and my mother would say it did not matter what had happened, he should not hit me. In the end we took our mother's advice: we could not communicate without squabbling, so we did not communicate at all.

My sister, on the other hand, was my best buddy and playmate. If I was given a teddy bear then she had gained a nephew. We kept our felt mice in a drawer called 'Mouse House' and they ate off Smartie-top plates and drove to work in a date box. If we played at anything for too long we would develop our own exclusive humour and everyone would moan that the girls had got the giggles again. When we were older we led separate social lives but we always got together to share the best part: the gossip.

Tessa was also a source of frustration. As a pioneer in character, I wanted to lead the way, but in everything from a Sindy Doll to a boyfriend she would get there first. Twenty-one months older than me, my sister could read and paint and dress better than I could. My mother would explain that my three-year-old hands just could not do what her five-year-old hands could. I was not satisfied. I wanted to be the eldest.

The other people in my new life were my parents, My mum was Mum. She would talk to us. She never put on a baby voice to do so, and reckoned there was nothing we were too young to know about. I have memories of being piled in the back of the car with my siblings listening to Mum explain the welfare state, or that she gave us pocket money not just so we could buy sweets but so we could learn how to budget and handle finances. My dad had his own business. That was what made him different from other fathers and why he worked so hard. He had Dennis Healey eyebrows and wore a suit like the men who read the news. Later I learnt he was a chartered accountant, and a Conservative city councillor and church-warden in his spare time. He was very frightening.

My parents met at their university debating society. They were thinkers and the intellectual discussion which had brought them together remained an important means of communication in the family. Meal times were not occasions when we all got together for a laugh or a gas. They were a forum for discussing entry to the Common Market or the introduction of VAT. Being asked to recite the six times table was as common as passing the bread and butter.

We were middle class through and through, from our emphasis on individual achievement to our company car, ponies and private schools. Daddy was a Tory and we were well off because we worked hard. People who voted Labour were lazy and gripey. We valued art for the sake of art, knowledge for the sake of knowledge, human dignity and private enterprise.

As a child I was rebellious. I was fiercely independent and continually frustrated by being inarticulate. I needed my solitude and hated family holidays because they meant I could not be alone. I never had to be sent to bed because my favourite occupation was being in my room with my book and my bedside lamp.

I was a feminist from my cot, though that was not how I described myself. I could not grasp 'oppressed' or 'stereotype' or 'status' or 'power', but 'not fair' was very much a part of my childhood vocabulary. One day I asked my mother how she came to have the same name as Daddy. She told me that she had changed hers when she got married. 'But that's not fair', I exclaimed about this ancient custom. On another occasion she explained that her engagement and wedding rings were a sign. 'What sign does Daddy have that he is married to you?', I asked. 'Not fair', I said when I learnt he did not have one.

It was the evenings that brought out my 'not fair' whine the most. The mere sound of my father's approaching footsteps would transform the home. My mother would jump up to put the potatoes on, my sister would change the television channel and my brother would throw the dog off the settee. I would run to my bedroom to find my slippers and do my dressing gown up. It was all change when the man walked through the door, and I resented not just my father but the male role.

When I was ten our class was set an exercise in which we

had to talk for three minutes on a subject of our choice. I chewed my pencil top as I prepared my speech and considered what was more important than anything else. I spoke on Women's Lib. I do not know where I got my ideas from but it was not my mother. She was converted to feminism only later through the adult discussion of my sister and myself. When we were teenagers she had no time for such nonsense.

School was a positive experience for me. I learnt how to read, add up and subtract, and that I was a clever girl. Apparently I was less evil-tempered at home because of the stimulus that the classroom offered. I remember enjoying my own world away from the family. After only a year of school it was decided Dominic and I would develop better if we were put in separate classes. School was even better after that.

When I was older I went to an all-girls school, where it was my friends that I valued most. I continued to enjoy the work but I mainly enjoyed being with Pip and Mary and Fi and Catherine and Vicky and Liz and Victoria. We roamed round in an eight and I knew then as I know now that some of these were relationships that would continue to grow for the rest of my life.

My only problem was the teachers, or rather my difficulties with authority. I spent many a lesson outside the door and was frequently told off for laughing too loudly. Recorded in my diary are the words: 'I must learn not to say what I think. It only gets me into trouble.'

The other significant feature of school for me was Christian Union. I joined CU when I entered secondary school for the same reasons that I joined the Modern Languages Society and the Scientific Society and the Junior Literary Society. I was keen and into everything – CU was one more lunchtime club to join.

I had never thought about Christianity before. My parents took me to church on a Sunday but nothing was said about it the rest of the time. Church was boring. It was horrible, like the dentist only it came every week. But at Christian Union I encountered something quite different from the accustomed stand up, sit down and drone of the vicar.

We met in a classroom on a Monday lunchtime and sat on the desks, just as we did in the other society meetings. Then a sixth former opened in prayer. I was embarrassed. It was the way she shut her eyes and pretended she was talking to God or someone. I giggled with my friend Fi who sat next to me on the window-sill.

It got worse. They started to sing songs and clap their hands as we had done in the junior school. To cap it all they began what they called a 'sharing time' where they told each other what God had done for them in the holidays. What threw me was the way they kept saying that God had spoken to them. I had never heard anything like it. Who did they think they were?

My curiosity was aroused, and I went the next week and the next. These girls had obviously experienced something that I had not and I wanted to know what it was. Eventually in a Bible study I asked the question that had been on my mind for days. 'You know you keep saying that God speaks to you', I said. 'Well, what does that mean? And why did Jesus die?', I threw in for good measure. I do not remember the conversation that followed, only that it left my questions unanswered. I decided to start praying myself.

I was eleven years old and did not know how to talk to someone up there as though he was someone down here, but I had no prayer books to help me either. I decided to write my own prayer and to recite it every night before I went to bed and every morning when I woke up.

So I would thank God for my mum and my dad and Tessa and Dominic and Ben the dog and Flikka my pony and for the eleven goldfish. Then I would pray for my mum and my dad and for Tessa and Dominic and Ben the dog and Flikka my pony and for the eleven goldfish.

Jesus presented a problem. I was sure that he ought to fit into it somewhere but was unclear as to how he came in. I would say, 'Thank you Jesus for dying for us, and I know that not many people would have been good enough to do that.' Then I would consider that many people had – in the Second World War, for instance. I hastily pushed the thought away as it was probably blasphemous not to believe that Jesus was special.

Another difficulty was saying the prayer once I had almost read myself to sleep. I would be drifting to and fro the land of nod before I got to the 'Amen'. After a few weeks of that delicious, snuggle-into-the-bedclothes feeling being ruined by guilt about not making it to the Jesus bit, I decided the time to talk to God was when I came in from school. Praying when I was awake was very different.

One afternoon I sat on the bed and began to run through my prepared order of words. For some reason I found myself stopping in the middle. I wanted to be still, very still, and just be. I closed my eyes and breathed in the silence. What happened then I find difficult to describe.

I sensed a being bigger than me, bigger than the world, bigger than the whole universe and yet intricately bound up in a part of me that was deeper than anything else I had known. I felt very special, very important. I had a role. Life had meaning. There was, there really was a God and he was better than anything I had imagined. The world was going to be all right and I was going to be all right. Everything would be all right because God was there.

I wept. It was the first time I had known tears of joy. I cried because a tender part of me had been awakened. I cried because something very deep inside was rising up and making itself known. I cried because I did not know what else to do. My experience was beyond words.

'Thank you God', I murmured as involuntarily as you utter the name of a loved one whom you hold. 'Oh thank you God', I prayed, and the more that I thanked him the stronger the sense of his presence became. I emerged from my room about an hour later with no language to describe it, just the awareness that something immensely significant had happened to me that day.

At CU they hugged me and gave me a language. In feverish excitement they told me I had been born again and become a Christian. Jesus was now living in my heart. Before, I had sinned and my sin had cut me off from God. That was what my life was before that Saturday afternoon. But Jesus had come and died to save me from my sin. He broke down the barrier between me and God and made those prayer experiences possible. Now, thanks to Jesus, I could hear God speaking to me. Now I would go to heaven. I was saved.

I continued to experience the indescribable in prayer. I got up an hour earlier to do it and started to read the Bible too. It was not that I was pious and certainly not that I was selfless. It was quite simply that at eleven years of age, with plenty of friends and a pony, praying was the most exciting thing in my life.

I was not yet at the age to find concepts energizing, so it was the person of Jesus who featured most strongly. I prayed in pictures. My first prayer picture was of a desert and I was struggling through it, thirsty and unhappy. I came across a man sitting on a tree stump all alone, looking into my eyes with his arms outstretched towards me. 'Jesus, I've been looking for you', I said as I approached. 'I know you have. I've been waiting for you', he answered, sitting me on his knee.

I had another prayer picture one morning as I lay in bed, worried about going to school. I imagined Jesus coming into my room, standing at the foot of my bed and winking at me. I smiled and got out of bed. No matter what happened that day, Jesus and I were in it together.

When I was twelve I kept a diary which I entitled 'How the Lord has helped me day by day'. In blue ink I would write down incidents and in red ink I would record how God had spoken to me through them. I had no difficulty relating my new-found faith to my daily living.

My diary tells of my struggles not to be jealous when Fi was wing attack in netball for the third week running, not to cheat in a Scripture test and not to be too upset when I only got a 2+ + for my Classical Studies homework. Answers to prayer were recorded. 'I prayed that I would not have any fillings at the dentist and I did not.' Some entries were disgustingly pious: 'I have decided to give up sweets for Lent and since then the thought of them has always made me sick.' Some were surprisingly original: 'The Old Testament is depressing because Jesus is not in it. Jesus was a very amusing person.'

It was in that year that I saw a television programme about a bomb that was let off in a pub not far from where we lived, killing dozens of people. The event is noted in my diary in blue ink. In red it says: 'Now I understand why Jesus said we must love one another. It is the only way. I must remember that all the other people are just like me. I am not the best.'

Faith added a new dimension to life. Prayer excited me, and giving myself a good hour each day to reflect on my experiences greatly enriched them. I had a sense of meaning and purpose. It also meant that I had a framework within which to place my thoughts, or, in my twelve-year-old words, 'It helps me know what to think about things.' It gave me some grip on my parents' intellectual arguments. If abortion was the subject of discussion I was able to say that God loved everyone, even unborn babies, and so we should not kill them. It was simplistic but at least I had a starting point, and that mattered.

I revelled in the inner independence from my family that accompanied my sense of God. They were not real Christians, so I believed, and it was my job to convert them. They went to the boring church up the road where the vicar used incense and kept cordially inviting us. He should have been sacked and my father should have been sacked as churchwarden because neither of them lived as though Jesus was real. Before long I was asking if I could go to the big, wild church a few miles away where it was rumoured they had a hands-up every Sunday.

I was not allowed to go. My father said I could not go because you went to your parish church with your family. My mother said I could not go because I was too young to travel on a bus by myself. I was furious that my parents had come between me and God. Eventually when I turned thirteen, after incessant nagging at Jesus as well as them, they gave in.

I put on my high-heeled shoes and make-up. I borrowed my sister's coat and turned the collar up. I was temporarily thrown when the bus driver queried whether I should be paying half fare.

The church thrilled me. It was a modern building and

Anglican, though this fact was well disguised. It was disguised by the people dancing in the aisles, the charismatic outbursts and the singing of songs all over again, this time as though we meant it. The first Sunday I went was the second after Christmas. We joyfully sang that Jesus had risen. We were real Christians.

I said: 'Hello. My name's Jo Ind', and relished the fact that nobody knew anything else about me. I joined the youth group and the choir and I taught in the Sunday school. I got on the hotline to God by speaking in a foreign language and waiting for someone to interpret. I took notes on the forty-minute sermons and I learnt great chunks of the Bible by heart. I went twice every Sunday for the next six years.

If I became aware of the presence of God over a few weeks, becoming a compulsive eater took a period of years. I can pinpoint the Saturday when I was first moved in prayer, but no one moment at which my eating grew out of control.

It was almost a part of growing up. Gradually in my adolescent years my interests started to change. Once playtime meant swinging or playing dens in the trees; it came to mean chatting and eyeing up boys on the cricket pitch. Once we thought our school uniform was uniform; it came to be a way of experimenting with fashion. Collars could be worn done up or loose. Ties could be wide and floppy or stiff and petite. Shoes would be platforms, then shoes would be flat, and the last to catch on was a square.

With this growing consciousness of our clothes came an awareness or our bodies. Sprawled on the grassy banks we would spend the summer lunch hours with our skirts hitched up to our knickers and our shirts tied in a knot under our bras. We would compare legs to see whose were the most hairy and discuss if it was better to use Immac or to shave. We would hold a competition to see who could get the brownest, and suntan lotion became the focus of our idle conversation.

We were growing up and searching for our identity as young women. We explored anything that meant we were no longer children and that distinguished us clearly from men. In our insecurity we reached out for the accepted signs, the ready-made hallmarks of who we were. The magazine culture of beauty, health and diets was offered to us – we eagerly took it on board.

When I went on my first diet it was not because I thought I was fat any more than I wore combs in my hair because it needed holding back. I bought a pair of tweezers and plucked my eyebrows, with more pain than success. I was given a manicure set and I started to push back my cuticles. My mother had a little pink booklet which listed foods on one side of the page and their calorific value on the other. My sister and I went on a diet together.

I had no idea how destructive it would be to know the energy values of foods. Before long I did not need the booklet because I had learnt it off by heart. I knew how many calories there were in a Mars bar, in a cup of coffee and in four ounces of peas. Lost was the innocence of eating what I fancied; gained was the guilt at satisfying my hunger. Once I knew that orange meant '50' and slice of bread meant '80' and more than 350 at a meal meant 'Tut, tut, tut', eating, even when I was not on a diet, was a matter of mental arithmetic and success or failure.

I began to dislike my body. My mother would say she must do something about her tummy, my sister would moan about the size of her thighs. A favourite phrase in magazines was 'perfect figure'. When I could look in the mirror and decide I did not like my bum, I was no longer a little girl.

There was worse to come. The calorie-controlled diets were followed by the grapefruit-and-egg diets, the all-fruit diets and the high-protein ones. I would go for four days eating just apples and oranges or for a week on nothing but chicken and fish. I broke my diets, of course, and I did it in style. I did it in the middle of the night, in the larder and in intense shame and guilt. I ate bread by the loaf, cereal by the packet. My metabolism was confused by such violent changes. Gradually I unlearnt how to eat normally.

I put on weight. It was partly because in the fourth and fifth forms I still had some inches to grow in height. It was

21

partly because my periods did not start until I was seventeen, bringing breasts and hips with them. It was partly because my eating was chaotic. Dieting was making me fat, and by the time I took my O levels I was clearly compulsive.

When I was in the sixth form a lot more happened to me than just starting my periods and my A levels. My last two years at school were ones of a shock, confusion and pain I had not experienced before. My parents very suddenly separated and then divorced.

My parents were happily married. Everyone thought so – my mother did, my father did, my brother and sister did, and I did; or rather, nobody gave it a moment's thought. Most of the time I was not conscious of my heart beating either. A few months into the first term of my lower sixth it was clear my parents were not happily married. More quickly than we could grasp, we had to entertain the idea that they perhaps would never be reconciled.

Divorces are messy and ugly businesses. People are not severed from each other cleanly and sharply as though cut with a knife; bones are crushed and gaping sores go septic. It is like being stabbed, and then before the wounds are healed being stabbed all over again, and then those same wounds being crushed under a mallet. The confusion, the toing and froing, goes on for years.

My sister and I would sit crouched in a room, eyes tightly screwed up, hands over our ears, wincing 'Shut up' as the house vibrated with the sound of our parents destroying each other. We learnt to climb out of the window. The only way of evading the intolerable pain was to get away from home. I would linger at school and stay as long as possible at church. I would walk home rather than catch the bus, window shop without seeing the garments on display – anything to postpone the moment of returning to the screaming and the crying or the tense, explosive silence.

Mentally, it was hard to keep up with the frequent changes of plan; emotionally, it was impossible. One week my mother was leaving and I wondered if that meant I was leaving with her. Then it was decided the whole family was to live happily ever after in another city. I told my friends and prepared for the wrench away from them – only to find it was all change yet again: my father, my brother and my sister were to move to another city and my mother and myself were to stay.

The chaos did not stop once that was decided. We heard Dad was bankrupt, then we heard he was not. He was to come back to work at the marriage, then a petition of divorce was being filed. We settled into a new, cheaper house, relieved to have a solid base, but then the solicitor told us we would move again. Dad cried, Mum cried, I ate.

I used to think it would be easier to have your own divorce than to listen impotently to your parents having theirs. I felt my mother's pain, and that hurt to capacity; I felt my father's pain, and that hurt to capacity. 'What can I do to make your mother happy?', my father asked, sneaking in one night when she was out. 'Where have I gone wrong?', my mother wailed, as I was awakened by her cries in the middle of the night.

What sustained me was my sister's solidarity. Dominic had gone abroad. Tessa was the only friend who needed no explanation. She described Dad alone reading Shakespeare, and I knew. I described Mum staring motionless, and she knew. Our stomachs did the same gambol when we heard the word 'affidavit'.

Other friends were invaluable too. They held out their arms to me when I ran out of the house and turned up in a heap on their doorsteps. I do not know what I would have done without my boyfriend Simon. He attended many performances of the great family drama. He took me out, he took me on holiday, he paid. Unlike anything else in my life he was stable, solid, and unshakeable.

My friends were indispensable, but at a deeper level I was held together by a sense of being loved that went beyond even the love that they had to give me. My secure family was no longer there; if we moved away my friends, my church, my school would no longer be there; but God always would. I clung to the rock of my salvation. I prayed to the one who was the same yesterday, today and forever. I had a theme tune in those two sixth-form years, a song I learnt at CU: 'Wherever I go, I'll praise him. Wherever I am, I'll praise him, for his love surrounds me like a sea. Lift up the name of Jesus, lift up the name of Jesus, for the name of Jesus lifted me.'

None the less I could not wait for the day when I could leave the family behind and set off for university. I saw it as three years of doing what I wanted to do, living as I wanted to live, studying what I had always wanted to study. I would be free and totally independent. For the first time ever in my anarchic life there would be nothing for me to rebel against. It was a naive optimism. I left home but not my greatest problem – I took my compulsion to eat with me.

It was in my time at university that I started to think seriously and systematically about feminism. All my life it had been a gut feeling, but I had never considered it philosophically or seen it as a political issue. I had heard of Susie Orbach's *Fat is a Feminist Issue* but never taken the trouble to read it. When I did it spoke to me with the authority of penetrating truth.

She was radical; she was original. She described in bold print the destructive cycle of behaviour I had been trapped in for the past three years. She assured me it was common and she gave it a name. She said compulsive eating was not just the cause of being fat but rather the symptom of some deeper problem. She pointed to the difficulties women have being themselves in our patriarchal society. She challenged me to throw away my diet sheets, to start to love my body, to find the reason why I behaved compulsively and to learn how to eat.

She made sense, more sense than any doctor, more sense than any women's magazine. It had never occurred to me that there might be more to my fat than my greed. I did not realize I had a recognized problem, with therapy groups established for those who need help. It was obvious there was more wrong than simply my inability to diet. She was right, she was clearly right. I should have taken her advice and vowed never to go on a diet again.

I did not – I dared not. What if she was wrong? What if I

got fat, really fat, even fatter than I was then? What if everyone else had some grand reason for eating compulsively but I
was just the one exceptional greedy pig? What if she talked me
into loving my ugly body? I would never make love. What if I
took her advice? I would never weigh eight stone again.

I kept trying to go on a diet to lose just a little weight
before I put her ideas into practice. I would learn to love my
body when I was thin; it was unrealistic to expect me to love it
as it was. I would listen to my hunger only once I had starved
myself a bit. My compulsive eating was deeply ingrained in
me – I could not let go of it that quickly. For another year *Fat
is a Feminist Issue* looked forebodingly down from the shelf
and someone else's chocolate ice cream looked temptingly up
from the fridge.

Truth always wins in the end. There is something unignor-
able about it. It does not need to make a loud noise; it whispers
and waits. When I had been a compulsive eater for nearly four
years I gave in. If I did not know by then that I could not work
diets, when was I going to be realistic about it? What had I got
to lose by listening to Susie Orbach? After all, I only had the
fantasy of being thin to give up, not the reality.

Very slowly I developed the courage and the conviction
to resolve never to diet again. I had to learn how to eat. I had to
be freed from my addiction. I had to love my body. I had to
find out why I was a compulsive eater. I knew it from my guts.

Another feature of my anticipation of university wonder-
land had been the Christian Union. I was sure I would be a
leader drawing lost and lonely souls to God. I imagined that
through the power of our intercession and our obedience to the
word, the Lord would perform miracles among us. God, who
was greater than we could conceive, would surprise us and
signs and wonders would be done.

The only thing I was right about was the surprise. The
Christians bore all the birthmarks of the born-again believers
I had known. It was me who was different to what I had
expected. I was shocked to find myself disliking CU; I was
frightened and horrified to discover that perhaps I did not
want to be a Christian.

At university I succumbed to the temptation of seriously thinking through my faith, and I found it did not stand up to rigorous scrutiny. I was challenged to meet intelligent and compassionate Marxists and agnostics and atheists. When I gave myself the freedom really to hear the creeds of my religion I found it deeply repugnant.

'You see those people out there', said one fervent Christian, pointing through the window at students chatting in the college bar. 'They're going to hell, they are, hell, because they don't believe in Jesus. It's up to us to convert them, you and me. They'll be turned over to the devil and what are *you* going to do about it?' Michael was not a madman, just the Evangelism representative of the Christian Union.

The CU was lead by two presidents, a man and a woman. In other universities the CU was led by one president, who was always a man, helped by a vice-president, who was always a woman. It had to be this way, apparently, because it said in the Bible that a woman could not have authority over a man.

One year the presidents issued a circular to all members. 'It is against the Lord's will for the girlfriends or boyfriends of CU members to sleep on the floor of their college rooms. If you have a girlfriend or boyfriend to stay you must book them into a guest room.' It was of course backed up by a verse from scripture, one about stumbling blocks, I seem to remember.

Six of my friends decided to live in a house together, including Fiona from my course and Peter from the Christian Union. Before we moved in, Peter decided to tell Fiona that Christians were very different from non-Christians and that darkness and light could not mix. 'Well in that case, why do you want to live with us?', asked Fiona. 'We are called to get our hands dirty', was Peter's reply.

If I had not been an Evangelical Christian myself I could have left them with their noses in their Bibles and charismatic experiences. After all, most people on campus thought the CU was a pack of loonies. Why was I still going to their meetings every day? I was still going to their meetings every day because for all New Jo reacted strongly against them, Old Jo still believed every word they said. Being hallelujah happy and

26

Bible-based biased was the only way I knew of coming to faith. This was what it meant to believe in the God I had known since I was eleven. I could not create a distance between the Christian Union and Christianity – if I abandoned them, I abandoned Jesus.

No one in their right mind, I reasoned, would look God in the face and reject him. It must be subtle seduction that gradually enticed people away. All this questioning and reacting was me following man's ways, not the Lord's. 'Come back, Jo', urged a trusted friend. 'You're running away from God. Come back.' In the second year I was asked to be a Christian Union leader. Wincing and kicking and screaming, I agreed.

It was good, if extremely uncomfortable. Having commitments and responsibilities in a society I could not stomach at least forced me to confront the issues. I had to help organize a mission. It was my role as a college leader to introduce the missioner to all my 'non-Christian' friends and leave it to him to do a better job than I could of converting them.

The missioner arrived. I could not admit it to him, but it was an enormous step to admit to myself that actually I did not want my friends to become Christians. What if they were to turn out like the ones that I knew? Christians seemed to be characterized by cagoules, three-chord choruses and fear: fear of disobeying God, fear of thinking, fear of being themselves. My other friends were characterized by colourful clothes, let-your-hair-down music and freedom: freedom to be who they wanted to be, freedom to question, freedom to let it all hang out and have a damn good time. If they were liberated without it I had no desire to offer them the bonds and shackles of religion.

The mission ended. Those that had been converted gave their testimonies, genuinely thrilled and excited at their new-found sense of the presence of God. I recalled my own happiness in becoming a Christian and the immeasurable, unquantifiable enrichment of faith in my life. I wondered if I had let my friends down.

The confusion continued. There was so much about this Christianity that I could not believe. That wives should obey their husbands grated on me as a feminist, and slaves submitting to their masters I found repugnant as a human being. It was ridiculous to suppose one group of people had a monopoly on the being who created the universe. It was especially ridiculous when you saw how dull the Christians were who claimed this. If it was only this tiny minority going to heaven, hadn't God made rather a bosh-up with his means of salvation?

In the end it was a tiny incident that brought about the day of judgement. I was at a Christian Union leaders' meeting where we were discussing the problem of Bible study members being stunned into an uncooperative silence once you had opened in prayer. 'Isn't the problem the opening in prayer?', I volunteered. The group looked horrified. 'Well you know', I explained, 'it creates the feeling that the holy bit has started so from now on everyone had better watch what they say.' I was told coldly that it was inconceivable to read the Bible without praying first and it was hoped that I never conducted my studies without doing so.

I left the meeting, went home and prayed out loud, very loud. 'God, just look what you are doing to these people. Look at them. They are small-minded, poxy and bigoted. It's not that they can't think, God, it's that they won't and do you know why they won't?' I screamed in frustration, 'Because of you, O bringer of life in all its fullness.

'I can't stomach you. I find you nauseous. Get out of my life. Jesus Christ, I'm telling you. Leave my heart. It's not that I don't believe in you, it's just that I can't stand you and if that means I'm going to hell then I'm going. It's the only place I can be with integrity.'

I sat cross-legged on the bed and calmed down. From my window I could see the cows chewing the cud. I was fond of the gentle, waddling, uddered mooers and had chosen my room so I could look out at them. I watched them bring up the grass they had swallowed so easily earlier and take the time to ruminate before it could be properly digested. I tried to work out where I was.

I was not committed to the Christian Union. I was not

28

committed to Christianity – I was not even committed to God. I was committed to the pursuit of truth. Whatever truth was and wherever it took me, that, not the Bible, was my bottom line. I had to pursue truth and see if it pointed me to God, not assume that God existed and that not to believe so was false.

Furthermore I had to trust my guts, my mind, my ability to think and feel, because they were me and it was me that had to do the believing. Of course it was possible that my brain was warped and my judgement distorted and that they would lead me into lies. But at the end of the day they were all I had. Even if I decided to obey the Bible, that would be a decision that my mind had made. Certainly I ran the risk of being individualistic, but then it was the Evangelical Christians who were so keen on a personal relationship with Jesus.

'God, if you are there, reveal yourself to me', I prayed. 'If I am so perverse that I am incapable of finding you then the onus is on you to make yourself known. And if there is nobody up there and I've been deceiving myself for years, then I'm looking pretty silly right now talking to the ceiling.'

So I began the process of radically re-evaluating my faith. I called it building a lighthouse. My rock or foundation was the fact that I could do no more than go with my mind and my guts. My bricks were very carefully chosen. 'Prayer changes me' was laid. 'Prayer changes things' was put to one side, perhaps to be cemented in at a later date. 'Only people who believe in Jesus go to heaven' was chucked with all my might on to the rubbish heap, and plenty more rubble was added.

The quest to discover what sort of god God must be, if he were to exist, had started. I could tolerate nothing that smacked of baloney, nothing that sounded hollow or false. It was difficult, confusing and frightening, like all the best adventures.

And it was in that same year that another quest had begun. I was finding out why I was a compulsive eater. I was looking into my guts and growing in touch with my feelings to discover what I was doing every time I binged. The means by which I came to these periods of exploration were quite independent. It never occurred to me that they were related.

I would never have imagined the scenario or anticipated what was to come. I had not guessed that prayer and stuffing my face could inform each other. I did not realize that my faith was to save me from my compulsion to eat, which in its turn would rescue me from the snares of my religion.

3

Everybody's somebody

Chocolate – it was definitely chocolate, and when it is chocolate nothing else will do. If you could do with a pint of beer,
you could manage on lager; if it is ice cream you want, then
mousse will do instead; but when you want chocolate, it has to
be chocolate. That is the way it is.

I was not particularly depressed or miserable. I was in my
first year at university, feeling the luxury of having too much
of a good time. I found my work stimulating, but there was too
much of it. I had some great friends, but I was seeing too much
of them. I enjoyed being busy, but I was getting very tired. I
needed a weekend away from it – that was all.

And then there was the problem of the college phones.
One had broken. That meant that there were only two phones
to serve six hundred people. I had phoned Simon three times
that evening but he had not been in, and I had queued for a
total of two hours just to establish that fact. So I needed to
get away, but could not make the arrangements – that was
all. It was just a middle-of-termy, mildly frustrated, nothing-
I-could-decently-moan-about,   ten-o'clock-Thursday-night,
chocolatey kind of feeling.

So, where could I get chocolate from at this time of night?

31

There was a machine down in the college bar. I could not possibly get some from there – someone might see me. I might be caught dropping a coin in the slot, pulling out the tray and taking a bar of chocolate. Everyone would stare – then they would know why I was fat. I would have to walk past them red in the face with my head down. No, I would have to rely on my emergency supplies.

I put a tablespoon of margarine into a bowl. I creamed some icing sugar into the margarine, stirred in some cocoa powder and there it was: instant chocolate – and in the same instant it was in my mouth and some more margarine was in the bowl, and so on. I do not know how many times I repeated this exercise. I was standing up lost to a sense of time or feeling. I might have been feeling sick, but I was not listening to my feelings. All that there was in the world was me, the margarine, the cocoa and the icing sugar.

Knock, knock, knock. The external world was making itself known. I became aware that the lid of the carton was margarine-side down on the table. A white dust and a brown dust were delicately sprinkled over all my books, papers and letters. The cocoa packet was lying on its side. The icing sugar packet had margarine greased over its inner bag.

Knock, knock, knock. 'Jo. It's only me, Fiona. Can I come in?' I grabbed the bowl, spoon and edibles with one hand and threw them under the bed. I put a book over the margarine patch on the table, blew the dust around, picked up another book, sank into an easy chair and said, 'Yeah, come in', in a nonchalant manner. Fiona put her head round the door.

'I only came to see if you were OK. You seemed a bit fed up in the bar earlier.'

'Oh sorry. Have I been a miserable old cow?', I apologized.

'No, not at all. No one else would have noticed. I just thought you weren't quite yourself', Fiona said.

I started to natter. 'Oh, I'm just feeling a bit middle-of-termy. I'll be OK once I get away. I'll ring Simon at midnight, get him out of bed if needs be. I'll be OK once I've got it arranged . . .' As I was talking I noticed that Fiona was looking at something. When I realized what she was looking at I felt my clothes being stripped off me, and I was becoming hotter and hotter the barer I became. There on my finger, directly in the shaft of her gaze, was a lump of instant chocolate that had been on its way to my mouth at the time she had knocked. I carried on talking, stuttering, repeating myself, hot, awkward and distracted. Fiona sensed my embarrassment and said, 'Well, I just wanted to check you were all right', and left.

As soon as the door was shut I crawled into bed. I felt seedy, disgusting, dirty. I felt as though I was a five-year-old child disguised as an adult and Fiona had blown my cover. I was paralysed by a sense of shame and humiliation. I climbed out of bed, found a loaf of bread and crawled back under the covers, tearing at the loaf with my fingers, eating in procrastinating mouthfuls. I would never be able to look at Fiona again, I would never be able to come before God again, or at least I would have to wait until I had lost two stone and won their respect. It was hours before I gained the courage to get out of bed, brush the crumbs away, get undressed and get into bed again.

With any compulsive behaviour, like becoming addicted to drugs, alcohol or gambling machines, a huge hurdle to overcome is the first one: admitting there is a problem. It is humiliating and shameful. It is hard to come to terms with the fact that you cannot stop eating. It is horrendous to imagine anyone knowing about it. It is easier not even to admit it to yourself.

I had taken so much stock in being a person who coped. I passed exams, I prayed regularly, people became Christians under my influence, I never got into debt – I was a responsible person. A large part of my self-image was being competent and 'together'. I was going to go a long way. That is why it was so hard to recognize that in a fundamental area I was not coping at all. In a simple, elementary matter like eating I could not control myself. Rather than admit I had a problem I would resolve to diet tomorrow. I had to, if God were to forgive me.

God of course hated sin. It was loathsome to him. I could avoid Fiona, stay out of her way, try not to see her, but from

God there was no escaping. I felt beyond his forgiveness because I had committed the same sin more than seventy times seven times. I was making a god of my belly, submitting to my fleshly desires. It could not go on any longer. It would all be different in the morning.

My faith should have helped me to acknowledge my problem – it was about salvation, after all. The cross should have spoken to me of the way of the vulnerable. Christianity more than any other world view or religion should have helped me to embrace my feelings of weakness, of helplessness and of failure. In fact my faith did just the reverse.

At the core of my beliefs was the gospel which was preached Sunday after Sunday. I knew that we all had sinned, that we all like sheep had gone astray, and the wages of sin was death. That was the bad news, but the good news was that God so loved the world he sent his only begotten son so that whosoever believed in him should not perish but have everlasting life. The Lord had made the punishment fall on him, the punishment each of us deserved, and by his wounds we were healed. In other words we all deserved to be crucified because we had not come up to God's standard, but in his generosity God had sacrificed his son instead so that we could go free.

That was good news indeed, but it demanded a response. There was something that we had to do to receive the benefits of salvation. It was as simple as ABC: if I wanted to know Jesus as my personal saviour I had to A, ask, B, believe and C, confess. I had to ask Jesus into my heart, believe that he was my saviour and confess that I was a sinner. So if tonight was the night when I had moved from the kingdom of darkness into the kingdom of light could I please come forward/raise my hand/see the preacher at the back of the church afterwards and he would give me a Journey into Life.

That was the gospel and I believed it. The words preached were that there was nothing we could do to earn the love of God, but the message I received was just the reverse. Whatever they might have said, the impression I gained was that there was something I could do to gain salvation and in fact if I did not do that one thing I would suffer eternal damnation. God's love did have conditions. If I wanted to experience it I had to turn my back on sin; I had to promise to obey him; I had to invite Jesus into my heart.

Fortunately I was all right because I had done that when I was eleven and had continued to do it every day since. I was OK, then. Or was I? Didn't the fact that I was a compulsive eater show that really I loved food more than God? How could I honestly say that I was repenting each night, for repentance meant to turn back – it was not just a feeling, it was a definite action – when I persisted in doing the same thing, the same old sin every morning? I was a compulsive eater, but I was not a compulsive eater. I would turn back on sin. I would return to the Lord, I would start my diet tomorrow.

The feeling that God's love had conditions was sustained in my growth as a Christian. For in giving my life to Jesus I was adopting a new culture and learning a moral code. We got it out of the Bible, or rather we thought we did. Walking more closely with God meant becoming stricter and stricter about the things we were or were not allowed to do. Holiness was about formulating a mode of behaviour and sticking to it.

When I became a Christian I learnt that marrying a non-believer was out of the question, but as I grew in holiness I realized that so too was going out with one, and close friend-ships had to be watched with particular caution. When I became a Christian I learnt that holding a seance was wicked, but as I got to know God better I realized that so too was playing with tarot cards or reading your horoscope in news-papers. When I became a Christian I learnt that sex outside marriage was sinful, but as I became more like Jesus I realized that so too was kissing until you had prayed together and made some kind of commitment. Furthermore, even imagining kissing before you had prayed together and made some kind of commitment was as sinful as if you had actually done it (Matthew 5.28; if you don't know it go away and learn it).

I wanted to know God more. I wanted to be close to him, to be holy like Jesus. This meant extending the ten command-ments to the nth degree and adopting a more and more rigor-ous code of conduct. It was as though the love of God was not something soft, warm, flowing and all-embracing but hard, cold, rigid, and reserved for those unfortunate enough to be chosen.

This was my environment, this was my faith; and it was in this context that I had to make sense of my eating disorder. Accept my problem? Love myself? Let my weakness speak to me? Work with my pain rather than against it? These words were simply not a part of my vocabulary. But not giving in to temptation was. Putting on the whole armour of God was. Dying to the flesh was a course of action frequently recommended.

I was weak and sinful and I could not afford to admit it. I hid from everyone, including myself. My eating took place in private. It happened behind the larder door, in bed, locked in my room, but never in public. My best friends did not know the problem and it would have been unthinkable to tell them. That was bad enough, but there was another difficulty. My eating disorder was affecting my relationships, because I could not acknowledge to myself or to other people what it was that dominated most of my life, and I could not give the predominant part of myself to them. All my inner struggles, anguish and strife revolved around food and no one, but no one was going to know that.

They could know the bright, bouncy personality, the competent analytical mind, the sussed-out and sewn-up faith. They could only know the outer shell, the husk of the frightened, despairing, struggling person inside. Accepting my eating disorder meant accepting the most fundamental pains in me, and while I tried to fight and cover up that part of me I could not live from the depth of it.

My faith not only prevented me from accepting my eating disorder but also produced in me crippling feelings of self-righteousness. It is not a contradiction that I who felt inadequate also had feelings of having made it. The two have the same root, for at the heart of both lies a contempt of weakness. I despised weakness – I despised it when I saw it in myself and when I saw it in other people.

There were some areas in which I was not weak, some

areas in which I was very strong. I was a Christian Union leader and I kept my life in order. I learnt a section of the Bible off by heart each week. Since the age of eleven I had given 20 per cent of my pocket money to the Third World. I spoke in tongues and one day I would be a missionary. Having a highly developed moral code worked in two ways: I was consumed with feelings of guilt when I failed but paralysed by self-congratulation when I succeeded.

It was not only myself that I evaluated in terms of the moral code, but other people too. I saw them through the perspective of the rules and regulations that I was conscious I had to obey. Where people failed to conform they reaped what they deserved. People who had casual sex deserved to get pregnant; those who did not work deserved to fail their exams; if you did not respond to the altar call you deserved to go to hell. I deserved to be fat.

One day in a moment of great depression someone asked me if I believed God loved me. 'Do you believe God loves you? Do you really believe at every level of your being that God is your loving heavenly Father?', she asked. I did. I did believe that, and on reflection I could see that it made my compulsive eating worse.

Everyone will have a different understanding of the word 'father'. More than most words it will be riddled with associations from personal experience. For me it meant hard-working, distant, the boss, and removed from the realm of my feelings.

In our home there was a definite division of labour. My mother provided for emotional demands, my father for financial ones. My mother stayed at home all day, my father went out to work. My mother's main concern was us, her children; my father's was his business, his employees and his customers. Of course there were areas of overlap. My father would look to my mother for advice in the business and he would sometimes play with us and put us to bed. None the less, 'Daddy looks after his work and Mummy looks after us' was the way the situation appeared in my childish perception, and that is what formed the raw material of my adult images of God.

As a consequence of this division, the strongest mental

picture I had of my father was of a man leaving the house. 'Father' meant the man wearing a funny hat and a suit with stripes like the toothpaste, a briefcase in one hand, striding off to do the unimaginable in a place I could not visualize. 'Father' was a man sound asleep in front of the telly, because he had had a hard day at work, while the rest of us watched the programme that only he had wanted to see. 'Father' was an absence and a presence working in his study. I could not see him but I knew he was there, and I knew I must not scream when my brother hit me or I would get into trouble for making a noise. 'Father' meant the one who works.

And so, because my father was busy earning the money to enable us to live very comfortably, several things followed. It meant my father was someone who was not there. When I was a baby awaking and crying in the night it was not my father that came to rescue me. At that all-important moment of twenty to four it was not my father that stood on the terrace ready to greet me, hear all my stories and glow with pride over my pictures and my model pig. My father did not know the names of the six little people that I slept with each night or that the doll's house became a lion with one ear in the dark. My father did not have time to become involved in my world.

My father was distant not only because he did not enter my world but because I could not enter his. I had no idea what my father did all day or in the evenings when he worked in his study. Every so often my mother would tell me that the business was going through a difficult time, and I would feel vaguely insecure and await signs of tension, but I could not imagine what this meant. When my father opened a new office by holding a party in it I ran up and down the corridors, played with the pens and felt a desire to be rude to the strongly perfumed people drinking horrible sparkling stuff that was not pop. The experience did not demystify my father's world – it seemed as distant as ever.

My father was distant not just because of his work but also on account of his gender. Unlike my mother he did not nurture me in the womb, he was not present at my birth and he did not breast-feed me; but there was more to it than that. I was never told but I always knew that I was the same as my mother but different from my father. When I grew up I would be like my mum whereas my brother would be like my dad. The fact that I looked more like my father and shared many of his qualities was irrelevant. I identified with my mother.

So God was father and he was busy. He was actively working out important things like salvation and atonement, but if I prayed hard enough I could arrest his attention. He was not intimately involved in our daily living in the natural course of events but only in as much as we 'offered it up', 'gave it to the Lord' or 'surrendered it to Jesus'. In this way it was possible to draw near to God from our position of distance. Of course I believed that Jesus lived in my heart as well, but I had no consistent picture of prayer to develop this idea. Prayer was not about creating the space for him who is within you to make himself known. It was about asking him who was outside you to make his way in.

Furthermore, I found myself trying to explain to God what it was like to have an eating disorder. 'God, I just cannot stop eating. Food seems to make its way into my mouth all the time. I'm making myself fat and you see God that's terrible because . . .' Basically I did not believe that God understood. Eating problems were problems with a gender – most compulsive eaters are female and God the Father was male.

Besides, I did not associate 'father' with understanding emotions. In our household it was not my father who mopped up tears by sitting us on his knee and helping us articulate our feelings. As I grew older and got to know other men, that impression was confirmed. Talking about emotions was not the strength of masculinity in general. We as a society have robbed men of their ability to cry. 'Big boys don't cry', we say to our little boys. 'Sissy, sissy', they jeer at each other. Grown men learn not to feel comfortable with their tears. They develop the stiff upper lip. Men go to work and in the world of work it is not the feelings that are the important things; it is the profit or the loss or the company's turnover. In the world of work people learn how to become professional, and a professional person is one who is able to perform well regardless of how he feels. In conceiving of God as father I thought of him as male and as above things as inefficient as emotions.

This was actually taught at church despite the belief that Jesus lived in the heart.

Feelings come and feelings go and feelings are deceiving
My warrant is the Word of God, naught else is worth
believing,

was an adage that I learnt at the age of twelve and repeated to myself for years to come. Only 'peace' was recognized as being an element of spiritual growth, and then it was emphasized that peace is much more than a feeling. I imagined that growing closer to God concerned learning to ignore my emotions rather than working with them.

So when I came before my heavenly father with an eating disorder I described it in terms of my outer behaviour rather than my inner distress. An eating problem, so I thought in the presence of my heavenly father, is the problem of eating too much and getting fat rather than the problem of self-hatred, inadequacy and a low self-worth manifesting themselves in destructive behaviour. The solution to the problem was to claim the power of the Spirit and exercise self-control, not to explore the feelings and listen to them. God took the masculine approach.

A further association that I made with the world of work and so with masculinity and fatherliness was that of respecting strength and despising weakness. In the world that my father occupied, the demands of the powerful took precedence over the needs of the powerless. Everywhere in the world of work, with the exception of an Israeli kibbutz or an alternative cooperative, there is a structure based on power. At the top there are the employers or the directors or the bishops, at the bottom the workers, the casual labourers or the unskilled staff. The people who are weaker, in whatever sense is appropriate, remain at the bottom of the power structure. If they are very weak they can be made redundant and sacked. The world revolves around the strong and the powerful. This is the way of the world of work and it was an association that I made with masculine values. Successes were valued above failures, winners above losers; women were not sorted from girls but men were sorted from boys.

In the presence of my heavenly father I felt more ashamed of my weakness, not less. I felt more of a failure than I would have done had I not been a praying person. When I saw God as masculine I saw the world as a hierarchical structure with the good people at the top and me, a compulsive eater, stuffing miserably at the bottom. God directed, God controlled, God would lick into shape.

When I was a child I saw a sticker on the back of a car saying 'Talk to God. She listens.' At the time I was shocked. I pointed it out to my mother and we agreed that it was blasphemous to imagine God was feminine. As an adult and a feminist at that, I retained feelings of uneasiness about referring to God as 'her'. But when I considered what 'father' meant to me, a solution appeared in my mind. What if God were my heavenly mother? For God was surely both male and female and neither, because God is a mystery. What would happen if I conceived of the femininity of God? If I prayed to my mother above?

When I imagined that God was my heavenly mother, the context in which I had an eating disorder changed. It is not an exaggeration to say that the whole world seemed a different place.

I realized that God was close, not distant. She was as close to me as I had been to my earthly mother in the womb, eating the food that she ate, breathing the air that she breathed, living within her, with her life within me. When I came to my heavenly mother and told her about my eating disorder I did not have to explain. I could rest in the presence of the one in whose image I was made. Worries about stretchmarks and thighs had a place – I pictured her as being on the round side herself. I took it for granted that she knew what it was about. Nothing I had experienced was alien to her. I rested in the love of one who knew.

My earthly mother was feeling-centred. Her job was to

listen to our emotions. She would sleep lightly so she would wake up if I cried; she knew the false tears from the real ones, the brave smiles from the happy ones. Disappointment, fear, happiness, excitement I would place into her receptive hands. If my best friend Fi had found another best friend or if my teddy bear's head had fallen off, she would listen to me, share it with me, understand me and feel it with me. She enabled me to handle feelings.

When I came to my heavenly mother with an eating disorder I found myself presenting the problem differently. It was not a matter of 'God, I'm fat', but 'God, I'm miserable'. Suddenly it was not my figure that was the all-important issue but my unhappiness. What was up? Why was I behaving in this odd way? What was going on inside? God was concerned with the root of the problem. The cause was of prime significance, the effect secondary. She cared about my sense of worthlessness, of self-hatred, of shame. She wanted to heal me from the inside out. She knew no magical three-stone weight loss would help me.

My earthly mother loved the weak. They were the centre of her world. When I was a baby she worked her routine out around my needs, not because I was big and powerful but because I was small and powerless. When I woke up in the morning and said, 'Mum, I don't feel well', she would cancel her arrangements, telephone the doctor, buy me magazines and ask me if I had slept or if there was anything she could get me. My mother did not despise weakness. She did not cut it off or dismiss it. She handled weakness by loving it, by loving it better.

When I came before my heavenly mother with an eating disorder I had no sense of shame. 'Success' and 'failure' were redundant words; 'winners' and 'losers' did not exist. I was a little child telling my mother I was sick. There was nothing wrong with that. In the presence of my heavenly mother 'weakness' was redefined. It meant the part of me that God was most concerned about. My inability to control what I ate was my poorly part, the part that merited extra fuss and attention.

When I was an Evangelical Christian I used to thank God

for loving me, the implication being that he was very generous to do so – it was not what we deserved. But I did not thank my mother for loving me. She loved me because she was my mum. She loved me before I was born. She loved me before she knew if I was a girl or a boy, regular or handicapped, pleasant or unpleasant. What could I do to escape her love? Turn up pregnant on her doorstep? Go out campaigning for the National Front? Nothing I could do would stop my mother loving me, because her love was not based on what I was like but on who I was in relation to her – her child.

So that was how my heavenly mother loved me. Could I undo her love? Would she become weary of my eating disorder? Would there be any point at which she would cease to know, cease to understand, cease to care? If I died of obesity would that make one jot of difference to her love for me? Could I stop being her child?

I realized I was loved anyway. I was loved despite, because of my eating disorder. I did not have to pretend I did not have a problem, I did not have to hide, I did not have to get a grip on myself, and quickly. I could afford to be open – I could relax a little.

It was funny, gaining weight at the rate you intended to lose it. It was amusing to eat a whole bar of chocolate on the way back from the shops and then seeing it labelled 'family size'. Nabisco used to advertise Shredded Wheat under the slogan 'Bet you can't eat three'. I could eat three packets. At one time it made me ashamed but later it made me laugh. It was a joke, or I was a joke, but it did not really matter because it was funny anyway.

It was not just Shredded Wheat advertisements that seemed different in the context of a heavenly mother. Everything did. I realized we are not governed from above by some masculine power, but nurtured from underneath by a feminine love. There was no power structure, no hierarchy; there was no ladder to holiness. There was just a world full of vulnerable people needing to be accepted and loved as they were.

And I was one of those people. I was a compulsive eater, hurting and in need of love, just like everybody else. My need of love was manifesting itself in the form of an eating disorder. So what?

In the presence of my heavenly mother I could afford to tell my friends about my compulsion to eat. When I did I discovered most of them had experienced some difficulty in their relationship with food too. I even found a few who were closet compulsive eaters just like me. In hiding from them I had been pushing away the love that was to become part of my healing.

As for the rules and regulations of my Evangelical faith, whatever was the point of them unless they helped us to love? God was not going to award prizes in heaven to those who had read their Bibles daily and resisted the sins of the flesh. He was going to make sure that the last were first and the first were last. If our moral codes and our religiousness did not make us more loving rather than less then they were, to use St Paul's words, utter crap.

God was not just my heavenly father but my heavenly mother too. I could admit that I had an eating disorder. My problem was more than becoming fat; it was to do with my muddled-up feelings that were causing me to eat compulsively. I needed God's love. I needed other people's love. I needed to get on with loving.

4

Fat body, thin body

They had gone in both knees at the same time. Two cheeky kneecaps were peeping out of my last pair of trousers and my spirits in empathy sank to join them. I was disheartened. This meant that I could not postpone the dreaded moment any longer. I would have to consider my body. I would have to look at my body. I would have to buy a new pair of trousers.

'I can't forget you because you're beautiful', the love-struck singer blasted in my ears before I had even entered the shop. Inside the sales assistant had similar emotional problems. 'And so he walked out. Just like that. After two whole months, he just walked out and so I said to him, I said . . .' I made my way over to the rails.

I passed the knickers that were sold as shorts, the bras that were sold as sun-tops and the pretty lace that was sold as bras until I came to the trousers. I had developed a method in shopping. First of all I looked to see if there was anything in my size; only then did I look to see if I liked it. I pulled the trousers back along the rail. Size eight, size ten, size twelve, size twelve, size fourteen. So there was a size fourteen. I held it up against myself to see if it would fit, but the waist resembled the size of my thigh. I moved on to the next shop.

The shops were always the same. The music was the same, the shop assistants were the same, the clothes were the same and the story was exactly the same. At the back of the rail there was a token size fourteen for fat people and even that did not fit me. I moved on to the same shop.

Two chain stores later I found a slight variation on the theme. It was a style of trousers that was loose and baggy with an elasticated waist. This might be the one. I eagerly ran the trousers along the rail through the eights and the tens and the twelves to the . . . but there it stopped. There was no fourteen. I found myself swearing out loud. I looked across at the shop assistants who were engrossed in conversation. I couldn't. I could. I couldn't. I could. I couldn't ask for a larger size.

I tried not to be intimidated but I found the prospect daunting. They were probably five years younger than me with five fewer O levels and a fifth of my opportunities, but they looked five stone lighter and that made them five times more powerful. I planned how I would ask, choosing my words carefully: 'Girls I am not worthy to dress fashionably, but only say the word and I will . . . run out of the shop as quickly as possible.' But no. I had nothing else to wear. I walked towards them for the sake of my exposed kneecaps.

'Excuse me.' The assistants were reluctant to disturb their conversation because they both fancied Steve.

'Oh, he is so gorgeous. You know the other day . . .'

'Excuse me', I said a little more assertively. 'Do you have these in a size fourteen?' One of the girls looked over her shoulder.

'No. We only go up to a size twelve with those. They're quite a generous fit.' I thanked them, waved my trunk, and left.

My spirit had sunk from my kneecaps into my feet and I trod them into the pavement. At the last shop in town I found a pair of trousers that I ventured to try on.

I never knew whether a hall of mirrors or a chamber of horrors was the best way to describe a changing room. Being in a room where there were mirrors on every wall, I felt like a vegetarian at a butcher's. I was joined by two carnivores.

'I must lose some weight', said one of them, patting her concave stomach.

'You don't need to', said Ribby, her friend, staring at her skinny body in the mirror. 'I'm the fat one. I want to lose a good half stone.'

'Well I want to lose ten pounds', retorted Skeleton Features, not to be outdone.

It is hard to hide in an open space with mirrors on every wall. I pulled the pair of trousers on as quickly as possible, shot one glance in the mirror and pulled them off again before the sticks could see. I looked enormous. I looked obese. The trousers had looked terrible and it was the last shop in town.

The shop windows were conspiring with the mirrors in the changing room. I kept catching sight of myself as I strode home. Every time I saw my body I recoiled in disgust. I wanted to jump out of it. I wanted to take a knife and slice parts away. I wanted to injure it. I wanted to be thin.

I bought a doughnut in the baker's. I ate that. I bought a bar of chocolate in the newsagents. I ate that. I went into the supermarket and bought a packet of chocolate biscuits, a packet of prawn cocktail crisps, a packet of dry roasted peanuts, a loaf of granary bread and a pound of smelly cheese. When I got home my knees dared to peep out of my trousers. I put my hands in the holes and tore the fabric to the top of my thighs.

There was no doubt about it – I hated my body. I could not even bear to look at it. It was disgusting, it was grotesque and it had to change as quickly as possible. I hated it because it was fat. I hated it because it was ugly. I hated it because I could not find clothes to fit it. I hated it and I ate.

As a Christian I was told that sin was loving someone or something more than God. There were three types of sin: sins of the devil, sins of the world and sins of the flesh. A sin of the devil was reading your horoscope rather than the Bible, a sin of the world was going to a disco rather than to church, and a sin of the flesh was compulsive eating. It was putting my stomach before my creator. It was making a god of my belly. It was loving me, my food and my body before God and his perfect way.

I believed that I loved myself too much. I indulged my

appetite, I was too absorbed in myself, I was pandering to my body's desires. I believed this was why I had an eating disorder and the solution was to learn how to despise the flesh. It was to see my body as being the grotesque lump that it was. It was to hate greed and fat so much that I never indulged myself again.

This was what I had been taught, and for years what I had accepted. But when I began the process of re-evaluating what I had been told I saw that it did not add up. The theory was that I loved myself too much – my experience was that I did not love myself at all. It was obvious that I despised myself. I hated my body. I could not abide my flesh. Whatever it was that was causing me to overeat, it was certainly not self-love.

If I did manage to look in a mirror I would sneer at the great white whale that stared back at me. I would stand side-ways and slump my stomach, seeing if it could bulge like an Ethiopian child's. I would punch my fat and recoil from my stretchmarks. I would systematically go through every part of my anatomy and find a fault. It was not difficult. Then I would tell myself that I had only myself to blame and I had better go on a diet tomorrow.

Whatever the theological doctrine I heard from the pulpit, two facts could not be queried: I hated my body and I was a compulsive eater. I was told that my disorder arose from self-love, but my experience did not bear out that theory. I decided to investigate what was happening every time I went on a binge. I decided to think it out for myself.

Maybe it was the hatred itself that was causing me to eat. Maybe my bingeing was not self-indulgence so much as self-punishment and deliberate self-abuse arising out of hating my body, and so I was overeating and so becoming fat and so hating my body even more. Maybe it was not my fat or my weak will or my lack of self-control that was the cause of my difficulties, but the very hatred I had so conscientiously cultivated.

After all, it was certain that I hated my body. And wasn't God love? Wasn't hatred nothing other than wrong, like a cancer propagating malignancies in uncontrollable destruc-tion? Wasn't it plain negative and crippling? If being slim was a good thing, how could it be brought about by hatred? How could a foul means bring about a beautiful, whole and godly end?

I hated my body and I was a compulsive eater. Stuffing myself with food was a form of self-abuse – it was the outward sign of my inner disgust. I was a glutton for punishment. Four years of body hatred was enough to prove that it did not reap thin harvests. I had to abandon the ideas that I had received. I had to say 'no' to my negative body image. I had to reach out in love.

Love my body? The very idea filled me with horror. Love this hideous lump of meat? Love the great white whale? How could I possibly love my enormous breasts, stretchmarked belly, outsize backside, flabby thighs, and solid, thick feet? I was too ugly, too big, too pale, too fleshy, too bulky, too fat. Love my body? Sell drinks on sticks.

That was the problem. To stop abusing my body with food I needed to love it, but how could I love myself when I was too fat? 'Too fat' was all I could see when I lay in the bath, passed a shop window, looked in a mirror or went to a party. One day I asked myself, 'Too fat? *Too* fat? Too fat for what?' My hips were too wide – but who had said so? My body was too large – but what did that mean? For the word 'too' suggested an element of comparison, some standard by which I was judging my body – but to what was I comparing myself? What was the criterion by which I decided whether I looked acceptable or not? My breasts were the size they were. What was I saying when I said that they were too big?

I was comparing myself to a woman who was introduced to me day after day. In the evenings I would turn on the television and she would be there, flashing her dazzling teeth in the American soap opera, making passionate love in the romantic film, washing whiter washing in the advertisements. If I walked down the streets she would peer down at me larger than life from a billboard. She would rumble past me lying horizontal stuck on the side of a bus. She would be sunbathing or painting her manicured nails between the pages of every magazine that I bought. Media Woman could not be ignored.

And I wanted to look like her. When I was assessing the way that I looked I was measuring myself in comparison to her. 'My hips are wider than hers' became 'My hips are too wide'; 'My breasts are bigger than hers' became 'My breasts are too big'; 'My thighs are fatter than hers' became 'My thighs are too fat.' 'I do not look like her' became 'I am inadequate.'

Media Woman was right – she drove the right car, wore the right perfume, seduced the right men. She had status. She was the ideal woman. She was the stereotype of sexuality, the epitome of good looks. Her body was constantly juxtaposed with the signs of success. No wonder I wanted to look like her. Were there many women who didn't?

No. Wanting to look like Media Woman was a common complaint. It was so common that there were magazines devoted solely to suggesting unworkable methods of losing weight. General women's magazines, that is ones bought by ordinary women, would always contain at least one feature on slimming. Up and down the country there were clubs established to encourage women in their dieting. In a survey conducted by a women's magazine it was established that 96 per cent of women had been on a diet.

I tried to imagine it – 96 per cent of women all trying to look like Media Woman. I thought of women all over the Western world bum walking, exercising to music, dancing with Lizzy. I pictured women counting calories, missing meals, and coyly patting their tummies saying, 'None for me thank you'. I considered women feeling inadequate, thinking their bodies were not good enough, not believing they were lovely.

Who was this Media Woman that had this power over us? Who was she that caused women to feel they were not up to scratch? She was a whim of fashion, the latest trend. Gone were the days of Renoir and Rubens's radiant, plump beauties; far away were the African cultures heeding breasts little but admiring enormous buttocks. Even Marilyn Monroe's figure was not in vogue any more. Today was the day of slim hips, long legs, flat chests and brown skin. We unquestioningly assented to the 'Be thin' command.

Consciously or subconsciously we were responding to

fashion. Denim jackets were in, and then denim jackets were out. Permed hair was in, and then permed hair was out. Once it was in to go in and out, and then it was definitely out. We lived in the age of slimming and we responded accordingly. When we wanted to change our clothes we went to a shop; when we wanted to change our hair we went to the hairdressers; when we wanted to change our bodies . . . there was a lot of money to be made.

The diet industry was a growth industry. More and more slimming goods were available to us and we did not have to go into a specialized shop or chemist to buy them. In a trip round an ordinary supermarket we encountered slimming bread, slimming cheese, slimming meal drinks. There was everything from slimming chilli con carne to slimming tonic water. Besides food there were exercise bicycles, muscle toning pads and self-hypnosis tapes. There were tablets to bloat your stomach before you had eaten and drinks to reduce your appetite.

This was the culture I had known and it had not occurred to me to look behind it. But when I did I saw the hidden commercial agenda. Women felt inadequate under the cult of Media Woman – 96 per cent thought they should change. Their insecurity was being exploited for financial gain. People were capitalizing on woman's discontent with herself. It was in those people's best interests to perpetuate the demand.

Picasso enabled me to imagine a different world. A friend had a print of his *Nude Woman in a Red Armchair*, painted in 1932. I nicknamed it 'Celebration of Curves'. The whole picture was of a delight in her roundness, the smooth circles of her hips, her breasts, her cheeks, her lips, her arms, her ears, her thighs. There was a softness in her voluptuousness, a delicious sensuality. She was undoubtedly beautiful. She was unfashionable.

I contemplated a culture in which Picasso's woman was the Media Woman. Suppose it was a curvy woman who sold us perfume on television, sprawled over cars to encourage men to buy them, demonstrated the latest kitchen equipment to cook perfect meals for hubby. Suppose it was a fifties-type figure that was pasted on billboards, decorated travel brochures, handed out freebies at the company's promotion. How would I feel about my body then? A lot better.

It was so arbitrary. One woman's figure was elevated above all others. Her body was not beautiful in an absolute sense any more than miniskirts were more lovely than maxis, curly hair more pleasing than straight. It was not that small-breasted women were more sexual than buxom ones, narrow hips more desirable than full ones, long, slender legs more attractive than plump, shapely ones. It was simply that the figure in fashion was thin, commercial interest kept it in vogue and 96 per cent of women believed their bodies were not right.

As I reflected on this it reminded me of something. It was a phenomenon I had come across before. Everyone was trying to attain some seemingly arbitrary standard being imposed upon them. People were not free to be themselves because of some false notion of how they should be. It reminded me of being a Christian.

As a member of a church and of Christian Unions I had developed a picture of Super Christian. She wore Laura Ashley dresses on Sundays and carried a Bible in her handbag. She did not swear or get angry. She sought rather than tried and ministered rather than got alongside. She went out with Christian boys but never felt randy. She was gentle and kind. The Lord answered her prayers.

For many years I was a leader on Christian holidays for teenagers. On one such New Year holiday I was unpacking and chatting to a fellow leader at the same time.

'I think you had better put those in a drawer', she said as I placed some of my belongings on a bedside chair. 'We don't want the girls to see them.' Jean was referring to a bottle of whisky, a Greek Orthodox icon and a book on feminine sexuality, which she thought would set a bad example to the seventeen-year-old young women we were responsible for.

'Honestly Jean', I said in good humour, 'I was only unpacking my Christmas presents. What would happen if I showed you what I was really like?' Jean laughed too, but I did hide them – and wondered how many other parts of me I was being asked to put away.

As Christians we expended energy discussing what it meant to be holy. We would decide it was being like Jesus and then try to formulate what this entailed. It certainly included going easy on the booze, not using graven images as an aid to prayer and remaining ignorant about vaginal and clitoral orgasms. But whatever it included, the discussion made me uneasy. It was almost as though there was some blueprint for spiritual growth. We were advised that the signs of falling away from the Lord were slipping out of habitual prayer times and out of giving money away. The notion of Super Christian evolved.

This was partly what caused me to reject the Christianity I encountered at university. It was the sameness of the way the Christians thought, dressed and behaved. It seemed that the more 'holy' they were, the more alike they all became. There was an implicit stereotype and they learnt to conform.

But I saw God as being the God of difference. My faith was informed by a very simple observation: whenever I meditated on the work of God in creation I saw that God was about variety. It seemed that whenever God made something he did not make it in one or two but in hundreds and thousands of ways. So God did not just make tea, he made all sorts of tea: Lapsang Souchong, Darjeeling, China rose petal and PG Tips. God did not just make beer, he made all kinds of beer: Timothy Taylor's, Landlord's, Darley's, John Smith's. He did not just give us language but all manner of different languages: ancient and modern, Romance, Slavonic, Hebrew, Welsh, Punjabi and Mandarin Chinese. And within these languages as diverse as societies themselves there was no end to the 'ta-ra-a-bit', 'see ya', 'good evening' and 'bye bye' of dialects, accents and regional variations.

The list was infinite. Whatever aspect of God's world I explored there were always kinds, and kinds of kinds, and kinds of kinds of kinds; different kinds of petals, schemes of thought, colours of skin, concepts of time, breeds of guinea pig, styles of music, senses of humour, types of planet; different cultures, different rain, different colours, different fabric, different alphabets, different light, different lettuce, different people. The world was bursting with God's abundance, from the solar systems outside our solar system to the atoms within matter, from the way in which people understood God to the spice they used in cooking.

I saw this as being God's glory. It was the effect of a God so immeasurable, so uncontainable, so loving, so imaginative and great that he could not contain himself in a colourless, one-dimensional world. Rather the goodness of God was such that he pulsated through every aspect of his creation, ejecting life in a bounteous abundance.

The love of God was so intimate and so personal that no earwig, no person, no cloud was the same as any other. The world was steeped in the irrepressibility of God. And yet we did not honour the God of variety. We enjoyed sampling various wines; we certainly liked having a wide record collection; we stood in a draper's shop and admired the different colours, patterns and textures of the fabrics. But we felt threatened by those whose skin was a colour not our own. Educated people despised the uneducated, who in their turn sneered at the urbane. The readers of *The Times* felt aloof from *Guardian* fans, and vice versa. Those who believed in arranged marriages failed to respect those who made love marriages, who did not try to understand the former. Christians saw different denominations not as a reflection of a God who is mystery but as a sign that we were not united.

So many of our problems arose out of failing to grasp the one who burst out in abundant variations. In our fear and insecurity we clung to our dreary sameness rather than rejoiced in difference. Super Christian constrained me. She hindered me from being myself and from accepting other people as they were. It put me off heaven when I imagined it as a place where Jesus dressed us in white, stiffly starched robes and lined us up round the throne in height order.

This was not the Jesus I believed in. The Jesus I believed in was one I saw in a performance of *Godspell*. He rescued those paralysed in sameness by making them more themselves. He gave the punk rocker another safety pin, he untangled the belly dancer's grass skirt and he restored the red nose to the clown. This was Jesus – not a Jesus who turned them into Super Christians but one who set them free to be who they really were. And the more themselves they became, the more different from each other they became. The big, gutsy woman became more raunchy, the humorous fool became more amusing, the elegant man became more sophisticated.

These pictures of God freed me to be myself. Holiness was about becoming more who I truly was. It was OK to say where I disagreed on doctrine. I could dye my fringe pink and tell dirty jokes. I could wear patchwork dungarees to choral evensong. I was most divine when I was most human, which for me meant being most Jo.

As I developed this freedom in my faith it spilt over into all areas of my life. For just as there was no such thing as Super Christian, so there was no such thing as the perfect figure. When God made woman, she did not just make one type of woman, one paradigm kind of body. That would have diminished her. God made each one of us different to reflect her rich and glorious image.

Some women undulated in sensuous curves. Some women towered in tall, straight elegance; some women peared with small breasts and large hips; some women hourglassed in a definite waist. Some women looked solid, robust and strong; some looked delicate, fragile and small. Women were dark, fair, clear-skinned and freckly-skinned, dimply and cheek-boned, hairy and smooth.

The variety of womankind was a reflection of the magnitude of God. It pointed to the love of a God who intimately knit us together in our mother's womb in such a way that no two bodies were the same. What was God thinking when we were all trying to look like Media Woman? Was God pleased? Was God laughing? Or was she hurting at the pain and the plain stupidity of women trying to become the body they were never given in the first place?

In International Women's Week I had a glimpse of heaven. I went to the gig of an all-women band to celebrate being female. There was Lisa in her round-rimmed glasses, dangly beads and hippy dress. There was tall Joy, thin and elegant in her dazzling trousers and shoulder-length earrings. There was Paula, never seen out of her jeans and denim jacket, pint in one hand, cigarette in the other. There was Clare, large and voluptuous with bleached spiky hair and faded Indian dress. There was Sheila, Media Woman herself, looking slim in her cords and pressed paisley shirt. And I was there too dancing with them, with bare, creamy shoulders and dove-patterned trousers.

We were all so gorgeous and yet all so different. I decided to be beautiful in my own way. I did not want to be the stereotype of good looks. I did not want to be the figure photographed, filmed and pasted everywhere. Why be beautiful in the established sense when you could do it in a way uniquely yours? Why was I trying to look like someone else when I could look like Jo?

I returned to the mirror. I had spent so many years trying to look at myself as little as possible, wincing whenever I caught a glimpse of myself in a shop window. It had been too long since I had stared lovingly at my reflection and enjoyed what I had seen. Not since I was a child had I looked with pride at the body that was me.

I had to learn to look in a new way. I had to change my criterion and ignore Media Woman. I knew how to love bodies. I had very slowly and gently peeled off a boyfriend's clothes, loving each part in turn as it was bared before me. I had seen his naked legs and chest. I had felt the bumps in his backbone and imbibed his warm, peculiar odour. My eyes had lingered on his limbs, absorbed in his loveliness. It never occurred to me to see how he compared to Macho Man. I was not criticizing each aspect of his anatomy as it was unveiled and seeing if it came up to standard. I was enjoying his body for who he was.

I knew how to love other people and this was how I had to love myself. When I looked in the mirror I had to learn how to see. I was not to look with a 'How fat am I, how ugly, how wrong?' but with a 'What does it mean to be beautiful in my own way? How does my body reflect God's glory? What is this gift of me? Am I voluptuous? Am I shapely? Am I generous?

Am I curvy? These are my thighs, my stomach, my waist, my breasts, my neck. This is the size of my lovely body.'

I needed help. The argument was convincing but I could not undo four years of body hatred all by myself. Anne believed that I was beautiful. She told me one day, and then she told me the day after that. In fact she made a commitment to tell me every day until I believed her. She wrote me a twenty-side letter expanding the theme and sent me cards proclaiming the same greetings. It was not just Anne either. Wherever I went, resounding in my ears was the 'Jo's beautiful' chorus. My friends never seemed to tire of the refrain. Liz took me clothes-shopping and said, 'You look lovely' to my wincing reflection in the chain store mirror. 'Jo, you are glowing, you are radiant', said my French friend Renee as she kissed me on both cheeks. 'You might think you're unattractive but that's not how other people see you', said Steve in his quiet and firm manner.

As I became more open about my eating disorder, other people told me about theirs. I was amazed at the number of beautiful women of all different shapes and sizes who said that they hated their bodies. I got to know some stunning women who believed lies about themselves and were made less effective as people because they could not see that they were beautiful. It made me very angry. Sometimes it made me cry when I saw the waste and unnecessary pain.

'What can I do', I said to them, 'to help you see that you are beautiful? How can I enable you to see yourselves as I see you?' I longed for them to love their bodies.

One day I shook myself. Wasn't I hating my body? Wasn't I believing lies and being made less effective as a person because I could not see that I was beautiful? And weren't beautiful women very angry, weren't they sometimes crying at the waste and the unnecessary pain? 'What can we do', they were saying to me, 'to help you see that you are beautiful? How can we get yourself to see you as we see you?'

How disrespectful dared I be? Would Anne lie to me? Was Jane indiscriminating? Could Renee ever be anything other than sincere? How long was I going to believe my own lies?

When would I be deaf to my words of hatred and listen to the voice of love?

I listened. I heard I was healthy-looking, with clear, fresh skin and a radiant glow. I heard that my shoulders were creamy, my boobs great and my legs shapely. I heard that my body was loveable.

And so I took my first step from my own self-hatred into the warm, liberating love that flowed from my friends into me. I leapt from the safe, suffocating bed to the exhilarating, freeing mirror. I was given the courage to move from self-recrimination into admiring my sensual body. I was graced with a desire to be Jo inside and out rather than a poor imitation of Media Woman. The foundation was laid from which I could stop punishing, abusing and stuffing my beautiful body, and eat in the way it deserved.

5

Body and sexuality

They were real men. The glossy holiday brochure was alive, talking, laughing, and virilely perspiring all around me. They had been working in the fields all day. Their grubby work shirts were stretched across their boulder-like shoulders and gaping open on their darker-than-suntan-lotion-advertisement chests. Their hair was thick and dark, cut close to their heads and decorating the rest of their anatomies in a manly abundance. As they ate their supper they slapped each other across the back, threw back their heads in laughter and opened their mouths to reveal their not-quite-swallowed food. I was in Israel; one European woman surrounded by nine real men.

I had been there for a month, which is how I came to know these Israeli men. As we ate our evening meal together they talked in English, just for my benefit. They were telling stories about picking fruit in the fields, teasing, joking and winding down. I had some stories to tell as well.

'. . . . .' One of the men suddenly started to speak in Hebrew. Everybody's attention was diverted to the other end of the refectory. I followed their gaze and saw it was eight Europeans entering that had caused the stir – or more precisely, the five that were women.

I had seen them arrive that afternoon and we had lain out in the sun and chatted. Two had come from Denmark, two from Britain and four from Germany. Some had travelled through Europe to get to Israel, some had flown direct. Some were students, some had grown restless in their jobs and given them up, one of them had travelled around from country to country for years, earning his living as he went. We had talked about their adventures, what their plans were, what they wanted out of life. They were a great bunch of people. I was looking forward to getting to know them more.

'. . . . .', said Yosef and slapped down his hand on the table.

'. . . . .', replied Renan, exploding into laughter.

'Come on guys', I said. 'Share the joke. Let me in on what you're saying.'

'Why do you want to know what we are saying?', Renan asked, looking me closely in the eye, a teasing smile on his lips.

'I'm interested. Go on. Tell them in English.' But they were too excited to be constrained by a foreign tongue, so Elan translated for me while the show went on.

'She is a good piece of meat.'

'I will have her, but I will wait until she is blacker.'

'Her breasts are too big. She would suffocate you.'

'I have been with bigger ones.'

'I am having a big one, right now.' There then followed a particularly vigorous display of back-slapping and my translator temporarily became absorbed in the banter. He carried on:

'These new girls are a fair swap for the ones that have left.'

'Those legs. Hey, look at those legs.'

'What I would like to put between those legs!'

'That is the one that I want.'

'I saw her first.' The men were aged between 24 and 35 years of age. They just about managed to resolve their argument.

'You had the first choice last time', said Renan.

'That is because the first choice chose me', said Zviker smugly.

'OK. You have her first. Then when you have finished

with her she can wash herself out and I will have my go', replied Renan.

I had held my tongue because I was intrigued, but I was beginning to find the conversation predictable. Nothing was to be lost by interrupting.

'Hey, Renan, Zviker. That is a terrible thing to say about a person.' The tone of the dialogue changed.

'Oh, we are only joking', Zviker defended himself.

'No you are not', I replied. 'You're laughing all right. But you are not joking. You always treat women just as you have been talking about them.'

Zviker found a weak point in my line of attack. 'We do not treat all women like this', he argued. 'Only the ones that we think of as . . . how do you say it in English? Sex objects.'

'Sex objects!' It was my turn to be animated. 'That's about the size of it. How can you call anyone a sex object?'

The men were bored with discussing the women by now. I was proving to be more entertaining. Large paternal arms descended upon me from all sides. 'Don't worry, Jo', they consoled me. 'We do not think of you as a sex object.'

'Good', I said snootily, my nose in the air. 'Because I do not want sex with any of you and I am certainly not an object.'

Encouraged that their remark had appeased me, the men went on to reassure me and to expound upon exactly why I was not endowed with the honour of this title.

'You are not a sex object. You are a friend', they explained. 'You make us laugh. You are good fun.' They made it crystal clear.

'And so I am not sexy? Right?', I inquired.

'Right', they replied. I had stated the obvious.

I felt asexual – that seemed to be what the men were saying to me. In my mind I had a picture of sexuality. It could be described on a bipolar scale. At the one pole were the sexual people. They were thin, long-legged and brown. Their bikinis were tied with cords at the sides. Their hips rolled from side to side as they walked. They slowly exhaled their cigarette smoke, pursing their cherry-glossed lips. They were cool, calm and emotionless. At the other pole were the asexual people.

They were white and fat with hairy legs and armpits. They wore swimming costumes. Their legs wobbled as they trod heavily. They did not smoke (lung cancer). They were sensitive and they would not play men's games. This was the picture that I had of sexuality and I was being told where I belonged – at the asexual pole.

I had said 'Good'. I had pretended that I was glad to be at the asexual pole. I had thought the men very disrespectful to the sexual women. I had thought it terrible to call anyone a sex object. I was not interested in being sexual. I was happy where I was, thank you very much.

But there was a part of me that did want to have the legs that the men noticed. There was a part of me that did want to be the first choice. If I was so glad to be at the asexual pole, why was I consuming most of my energies dieting and sunbathing my way to the sexual one?

But then what went with being asexual? Being a friend. Making people think. Being fun to be with. What went with being sexual? Being an object. Being a fair swap. Being had by one man and then washing yourself out so you could be had by another.

How would I feel if someone had said that about me? I would feel as though my intrinsic tenderness had been violated. I would feel as though someone had read my private letters uninvited, or as my mother felt when our house was burgled and her engagement ring was stolen. I would feel as though in even entertaining the idea someone was taking from me something precious, tender and intimate and making of it something valueless, something meaningless, something less than me.

The part of me that did not want to be sexual was angry. A part of me wanted to scream. It wanted to shake the burly men by their bronzed, muscular shoulders and beat their handsome, brown-eyed heads against a brick wall. 'Yes, but what about me?', I would cry. 'What about my poetry? What about my humour? What about my ability to reflect and make sense of the world?' One part of me wanted to act with such drama. Another part of me wanted to lament pathetically, 'Oh, why doesn't anyone fancy me?'

And so I realized that I felt ambivalent towards my sexuality. I had mixed feelings – I felt confused. While one part of me was fantasizing about being a stunning sex symbol, another part of me was clinging to my fat, hairy legs for all I was worth.

Gradually I began to understand that this ambivalence towards my sexuality was part of the cause of my eating disorder. It is very difficult to speak with authority about what is happening in the subconscious. To be conscious of one's own subconscious is a nonsense. But I believe that while all I was conscious of was wanting to be thin, subconsciously I was making myself fat. The battle that I experienced between the part of me that wanted to diet and the part of me that wanted to binge represented the conflict between my desire to be valued for being sexy and my need to be valued as a person.

Slurping my way through my breakfast cereal, crunching my way through crisps and oozing my way through cream cakes, I was rejecting my sexuality. Resolving to go on a diet and going to school on a grapefruit, I was trying to become more sexy. The battle was about more than my appetite, and I knew which side was winning.

And I had further reason to feel ambivalent about my sexuality. It was not just because I felt that to be sexual was not to be seen as a person; it was also because I did not like playing the feminine role. As I was growing up and learning about relationships between men and women, it seemed that there were common patterns in their ways of relating. Each assumed a position or a gender role and played their part in the sexual game.

The first job that I had was as a casual worker helping to sort the Christmas post in the Post Office. I made friends with some of the other female casual workers and we would all work together in a group. The gaffers, the people in authority over us, were without exception men. They were men, we were women, we started to play our sexual roles.

When we arrived in the morning the men would say 'Good morning girls' and comment on how pretty we looked that morning or how good we looked in jeans. They were pleasant and complimentary and we would look at each other, blush coyly and giggle. The men would then consistently pay us attention throughout the day. When we came across a letter that was poorly addressed we had to appeal to the gaffer for help. He would enjoy coming over, expressing his benevolence in assisting us by draping an arm around our shoulders as he placed the letter in the appropriate pigeonhole. At break the men would ask us to sit with them in the canteen, buy our coffee for us, and bit by bit ask us individually to go out with them in the evening. It was more interesting than sorting letters. We were playing the sexual game.

And I was good at it. I would tease the men and wait for the hand to descend on my backside. I would accept the offer to have my coffee paid for and succeed in persuading them to pay for my lunch too. When I sent a batch of letters addressed to Cardiff on the train across the sea to Ireland, I smiled sweetly, looked one of them in the eye adorably and got away with being thought cute. I knew how to be feminine.

I had more than my fair share of attention. I should have enjoyed it, shouldn't I? I should have felt flattered, shouldn't I? So why was there a part of me – at times a small part, at times a predominant one – that found it all rather patronizing?

For I did find it patronizing and the reason for it was that in even playing the game I was attributing power to the men. The basic ground rule of the sexual game was that the men were in the position of power and the women were not. The men were older than us, they were in positions of authority over us, they knew the job better than us, they had more money than us. They had power over us, and this is what made the game work.

If the roles had been reversed we would not have been able to play the sexual game. If the women had been older, in authority, better paid and in control, the men would not have found us sexy. They would not have pinched our backsides as we walked up and down – they would not have dared. If we had offered to pay for their coffee they would have felt humiliated. It is hard to imagine how we would have flirted under those circumstances. The men would have been impotent.

And of course it was not just in the Post Office that men had power and women were powerless. When I was a little girl growing up, it did not take me long to work out that almost all jobs involving status and authority were occupied by men; men were politicians, men were judges, men were company chairmen, men were fully ordained clergymen. When I was a little girl I absorbed the information that if I were to be a truly feminine woman, I would become a nurse, a secretary or a telephone receptionist. I would not be a politician, I would not make it big in business, I would never wear a dog collar and I would not have power.

My difficulty was that I did not feel powerless. Even as a child I did not want to be a demure, compliant female who took her orders from a man. I felt intelligent, gutsy and strong. I felt unfeminine.

So I associated my sexuality with not being valued as a person, I associated my sexuality with being powerless, and finally I associated my sexuality with sin. For the church provided a third negative picture of what it is to be sexual, a third reason to regard my sexuality with ambivalence.

The most striking feature of the church concerning sexuality was its holy, could-hear-the-incense-rise, concerned-with-things-of-heaven-not-of-earth silence. There was a deathly taboo, a formidable hush-hush. It was a silence made all the louder for the noise of the rest of the world. For elsewhere in the world people have enough to say about sex. It is dramatized in soap operas, wailed about in Covent Garden operas, sung about in most pop songs, featured in nearly all advertising, joked about in pubs and done before your nose at parties, in cars parked in lay-bys and in the alley at the back of the house. Talking about sex and laughing about sex seemed to be acceptable in every other area of life, but it was not something we did in church. In some ways it was a refreshing change. But the effect of the world's noise about sex set against the church's silence on the matter was that I came to associate sexual activity with the absence of God, and God with the absence of sexual activity.

Of course every so often the church did speak about the

actual act of sex. When she spoke she made big, bold state-
ments about it. She had something to say about sex outside of
marriage: 'Don't'; about sex with people of the same gender:
'Don't'; and in private conversations with the youth group
leader, or in a secretly read book, she had something to say
about masturbation: 'Don't'.

As an Evangelical Christian, whenever I heard sexual
desire described it was in terms that were negative not positive.
It was talked of in terms of lust and of sins of the flesh. Sexual
desire, we were warned, led to fornication, to committing
adultery. The emphasis was on being in control, on not giving
in to temptation. There was no celebration of the goodness and
the godliness of sexual desire, just of its need to be curtailed
and constrained.

When I was twelve I discovered that if I put my hand
between my legs it gave me a nice feeling. My first orgasm
came as a delicious, exciting, frightening shock. I had no
expectations of such a thing happening and had not even
worked out that my feelings were sexual. I thought I was the
only person in the world who had experienced this strange
phenomenon. I had never heard of masturbation. When I did
hear of it, several months later, I was horrified and disgusted.
Not only was I having sex before marriage but I was having sex
with myself, often as frequently as three times a day. I felt
guilty, grubby and ashamed. The following year I resolved
to give it up for Lent. I had failed by the evening of Ash
Wednesday.

Five years later I fell in love with Simon, a gentle and
loving man with whom I went on to enjoy a solid, committed
relationship. He had become one of my closest friends even
before we started to get to know each other sexually. And yet
my Christian conditioning was so strong that whenever we
ventured to explore ourselves anywhere between the thighs
and the waist, Simon would feel warm and happy about our
growing trust and intimacy, and I would get on my knees and
tell God I was sorry.

Sex, to me, meant sin, not being valued as a person, and
being oppressed. Furthermore, 'sex' meant 'thin'.

At some level, therefore, making myself fat provided a solution to the dilemma I faced as a randy woman unable to let go into her sexuality. In becoming fat I was saying to people 'Don't just gawp at my body. Take a look at what's inside.' In becoming fat I was saying 'Don't treat me like a baby. Recognize me for being strong-willed, independently minded, ambitious, determined, capable, powerful.' In becoming fat I was saying to myself, 'Don't sin. Steady on there. Don't get carried away. Don't give in to fleshly passions.' My fat was useful to me.

If I was to stop eating compulsively I had to deal with my subconscious need to be fat. I had to come to terms with my sexuality. I had to embrace it and claim it as my own. I needed to say a complete 'yes' to being sexual at every level of my being.

Ironically it was the Roman Catholic church, with all its quirks and hang-ups, which helped me to do this. When I was abandoning Evangelical Christianity I would go church-hopping, surveying strange congregations with my arms crossed, ready to run out before being spotted by the vicar. It was when I was maintaining a wary distance in the back pew of a Roman Catholic church that I was struck by a startling reference made to the sexual behaviour of its most revered saint. To me not having heard it before, attaching the word 'virgin' to the name 'Mary' seemed so incongruous that I sat and giggled while everyone else had their heads bowed in fervent intercession. It seemed like introducing a group of people, saying, 'This is Michael – sex every second night within marriage. This is Clare – unsatisfactory sexual relations with men, currently experimenting with women. This is Mary – virgin, and this is Richard – sex with as many different people as possible.'

As I became more aquainted with Catholic thought it seemed to be consistent, at least. After all the church was fond of virginity. All the best people seemed to be virgins. Jesus was celibate and so was the Pope. Being a virgin was a kind of status symbol, like having an OBE attached to your name. From my position on the outside looking in, I could see the messages the church must be giving to its flock. Whatever its

official teaching might have been, what it was actually communicating was clear: that God was better pleased with virgins
than with those who made love twice a night and thoroughly
enjoyed every minute of it.

Put so starkly I could see that this was ridiculous, but
what is more I could see that I had received exactly the same
message from my quite different tradition. The Catholics and
the Evangelicals used different language and recognized
authority in different places, but their fear and its effect were
the same. The Catholic church had celibate men at its head, the
Evangelicals preached on the sins of the flesh. The Catholics
venerated Mary Ever Virgin, but who was I to sneer? The
image of God that I had inherited was not exactly bursting
with phallic energy either.

Gradually I began to have a fresh image of God, a new
vision that helped me embrace my sexuality and made me glad
to be horny. Again, ironically, it was in a Roman Catholic
monastery that I was helped to make the connection between
the sublime and the sexy.

The monastic church was modern, in fact it was still being
built. From the outside it looked like a space-ship dropped into
the countryside. On the approach all that could be seen was
scaffolding, a windowless wall of bricks and an upturned
saucer for a roof. Inside there was nothing; vast expanses of
nothing between the mighty pyramid pillars, between the
sloping ground and concrete, circus-ring ceiling. There was
nothing on the altar, nothing on the yellow brick walls,
nothing on the floor but a dull, pile-less carpet. There was
nothing to taste, nothing to smell, nothing to hear.

There was a thick, inviting silence. Distilled prayer was in
the air.

I would sit literally for hours, leaning against the back,
left-hand pillar, inwardly unpeeling in response to the naked-
ness of the building. Just being there felt like prayer. It was
enough to sit or lie, absorbing the sense of the presence of God
communicated in the stillness, in the space and in something
else unknown.

The roof was a mighty wheel, its diameter almost the

width of the entire building. Its huge circumference rested on the eight plain pillars spaced around the edge. The spokes of the wheel were myriad concrete arms reaching out to the limits, the rim, and connecting all that is to the paradox, the hub. There at the convergence was a concrete cylinder beaming shafts of light into the womb of the church. There at the convergence was a concrete opening, glimpses of the sky, aperture of beyond.

I would be drawn to look at the roof at the point at which the monks sang the beautiful song from Colossians:

He is the image of the invisible God,
the first-born of all creation;
for in him all things were created,
in heaven and earth, visible and invisible.
All things were created through him and for him;
he is before all things, and in him all things hold together.

As I listened to these words and looked at this roof, feeling stripped in the bareness of the building, a very sexual picture of God emerged.

I saw God as huge. Big like the outer concrete ring, bigger than anything I could think of and therefore bigger than the Bible, bigger than religious meetings, bigger than the church. He was bigger than Christianity, he was bigger than the world. Through Jesus everything that was not Jesus himself (cups of coffee, tropical rain forests, Asian culture, logical positivism, dreadful jokes) had been made. In Jesus everything that there was in this world was held in arms like spokes containing all creation, pointing to its source, its centre, its light, beyond.

I saw that God was in the exhilaration of riding a motorbike fast round a deserted Greek island with the wind streaming through my hair and the sun beating against my bare arms and legs. I saw that God was in the laughter in that unexpected moment that slides people off their chairs, wobbles them like jelly on to the floor and sends a delicious almost-pain through the stomach. I saw that God was present in the group of sweating people pressed to the front of the concert stadium, their hands raised above their heads, swaying from side to side united in the atmosphere of hearing a band live.

I saw that God was waiting for me in my room with the open fire, the candles, the incense and the rugs on the wall, in the slow jazz music and the soft, well-worn cushions. I saw that God was in the wonder when a poem is understood and a new insight into the world is made as thoughts and emotions have been encapsulated in words by a fellow traveller, a kindred spirit. I figured that if Jesus was the agent of all creation, he was at least in those things that I loved most. I sensed the sensuality of God.

I saw God as being and energy, the energy of creative and redemptive love. I saw that God was not static and stationary but dynamic and active. I saw that creation did not stop in the first chapter of Genesis and redemption did not stop in the last chapter of Matthew, but that the world was continually being created and redeemed in the passionate love affair between the three members of the Godhead. I saw that all of life had but one source, God, and what is more that source was in me.

And when I prayed in this way I realized that there was no difference between the sacred and the secular, between the worldly and the Godly. We lived in a universe, made by one, vibrating as one and held in one. When I prayed in this way I realized I did not have to choose between the spiritual and the sexual. In fact I sensed a point in creation at which the distinction ceased to exist.

I sensed God as phallic and erotic; bursting with the seeds of life, overflowing with creativity, and penetrating to the depths of me. And in the depths of me, I opened and said 'yes'.

I had caught a glimpse of the sexuality of God. Now I could leave those Israeli men to their back-slapping. For them sex was about status, brown legs and erogenous zones. They were easily aroused and just as easily satisfied; they chose not to integrate the movement of their genitals with what was happening in the rest of their beings. This was their choice – it was not mine.

As for femininity, I decided that I, as a female, was the best authority on what being female means. As a female I must become more 'feminine' as I became more myself, by very definition. If in becoming more myself I discovered that I was not compliant, demure and powerless but challenging, gutsy and powerful, then that was not my problem. The problem was in the stereotypical notions that did not reflect the richness of all that femininity entailed.

Finally, my own deep sense of being sexual was consolidated in meeting a man with whom I felt so much myself that society's notions of how women should look and behave became boring and irrelevant. David was sexy, vital and penetrating. He lived from deep energies that helped me to perceive the pulsating energy of God, the world charged with the grandeur of God. He was integrating his sexuality with his spirituality and it was therefore possible for me to make an integrated response to him.

In doing that my own deep sense of being sexual was confirmed. I no longer needed to cling to my fat to protect me. I could let go. Being shapely and sensuous and sexy was not something alien reserved for the sinful. It was my response to an erotic God, erotic people and an erotic world.

6

Body versus spirit

I had one leg on the loo seat, the other was on the floor. I was doing it because I was a twentieth-century woman, I was doing it because it was the key to freedom, I was doing it because all my friends had done it. I was inserting my first tampon.

'Come on Jo, you can do it', I told myself. 'You can do it. You've got to do it.' My eyes were screwed up and I was tense all over because I knew how important it was to relax. 'If you can't even manage with a slender tampon how will you manage with a super one? And if you can't manage with a super tampon, you'll never get on with a penis.' I gave up and sat on the loo for a rest. 'The problem with you', I told myself, 'is that you aren't really relaxed, you're tense. The problem with you', I corrected myself, 'is that really you are downright petrified.' So I talked to myself in calm, rational terms in an attempt to analyse the situation. 'Right, so you are frightened, now what are you frightened of?' I inhaled and exhaled slowly, trying to locate a cause for my fear. Basically I was afraid of getting the wrong hole.

This actually, however ridiculous it might seem now, was a perfectly justified fear. I did not know that it is impossible to insert a tampon in the urethra because it is only the size of a pinhead – no one had told me that when we had 'done it' in biology. All I knew from labelling the *Homo sapiens* (female) and from the diagram in the tampon box was that a woman had two holes 'down there', and I could not see what I was doing. Suppose I was the first person ever to have a tampon removed from her bladder?

With cool and calculated reasoning such as this, I realized the folly of my ways. I was like a person trying to find her way in a strange town without ever taking her eyes off the map, but if the map was to be of any use I had to look at the town too. The clearest diagram cannot be used unless it is related to that which it describes. I had thought that I could insert a tampon without looking at myself, by studying the picture alone. I bent over double as I sat on the loo in an attempt to sneak a peep, but it was no good: I could not see. This would have to be a full-scale operation involving a bicycle lamp and a mirror.

I felt as though I was doing something wrong. I should not be looking at myself 'down there' any more than I should look at my Christmas presents stored on top of my parents' wardrobe. I felt the need to justify an exploration of my body. I was not doing it for its own sake, of course, and I was certainly not doing it for some cheap sexual interest. I was doing it because I had to do it if ever I was going to wear tampons. Satisfied that my motives were pure, I propped the mirror against the bed, took one last look at the diagram and slowly opened my legs.

I had never seen anything so disgusting in all my life. It was not like that in the line diagram. It was a nasty shock. Well, in some ways it was like the line diagram, only it was not in nice clean lines. What I could see in the mirror was red and swollen and moist and slimy and yuk. I shut my eyes quickly and resigned myself to a life of adult nappies. Nothing was worth examining that.

My hatred of my body was deeper than just despising it because it was fat. It arose at a more fundamental level than rejecting whatever size or shape I happened to be. I found my labia disgusting simply because they were labia. I hated my body because it was a body.

As a compulsive eater I had lost touch with my appetite. I

could not tell whether I was hungry or not, I was no longer listening to my body's signals, I had no idea if I needed food. I just ate. Normal eaters were in tune with themselves. They did not eat by counting calories, they ate by responding to the feelings in their stomachs. If they felt the odd rumble, a slight feeling of weariness, a drained emptiness, they needed food. If they felt bloated, uncomfortable and weighed down, they knew they had had enough.

I did not. I had to relearn the sensations of 'hungry' and 'full up' by listening to what my body was telling me. When I had dieted I had purposely ignored my tummy's messages. It did not matter how faint or queasy I felt, I was allowed nothing until four o'clock, when I could eat half a banana. When I had binged I had purposely ignored my tummy's messages. No matter how great my surplus of undigested food I would ram in more bread, more cereal, more cake to serve me jolly well right.

It followed that the solution to my chaotic eating was not to go on yet another diet and become even more out of touch with my body. It was to listen to its messages, respond to its signals. 'Am I hungry?' was the way to normal eating. I had to abandon the destructive notions of what I should or should not eat and hear what my stomach was telling me. I was healed not when I succeeded in consuming nine hundred and ninety-nine calories each day but when I could eat because I was hungry and stop when I was satisfied.

Put like that it sounded simple. It was far from simple. Susie Orbach in *Fat is a Feminist Issue* first suggested the idea to me, but it was a long time before I had the courage to put it into practice. The main obstacle preventing me from eating what I wanted to eat was my profound distrust of my body.

When I had tried to insert a tampon and seen my vagina for the first time I was disgusted. When I cycled to see a friend on a hot summer's day arriving with a wet fringe and damp patches under my arms, I thought I was foul. I longed for heaven where I would not have a body. I could not believe that my stomach rather than my head would lead me into wholeness. I hated my body. I did not respect it.

74

I thought that if I began to eat what my body suggested I would never stop eating. I would live in the larder for the rest of my life, too fat to get out of the door. I would lie in bed, too large to roll over, my only exercise being the movement of my jaws as I ate raw cake mixture, garlic bread and chocolate fudge cheesecake all day and all night. I thought my appetite was limitless, my body insatiable. At first I would not even dare to try.

This was the crunch, a conflict that had to be resolved before I could learn to eat. If I accepted that my body was good and its messages reliable, I could dare to listen to them and stop behaving compulsively. While I continued to believe that my body was grotesque, I never would be able to.

Heather reminded me that I had not always hated my body. She was five years old and one of her favourite games was to reconstruct the dinosaur age in the bath. One day as I watched her play she turned to me, placing her hands firmly on her absence of hips. 'I like my body', she said. For Heather it was as natural as enjoying the water, the bubbles and the plastic monsters. For me it seemed impossible.

I asked myself what had gone wrong. What had changed me from being a person who enjoyed playing in the bath with nothing on to a person who could not bear to look at her body? What had changed me from a person who ate when she was hungry to a person for whom 'hunger' was a meaningless word? What had changed me from a person who could say 'I like my body' to a person who fantasized of an existence without one?

Part of it was the culture of adolescence, in which changes to the body are viewed with suspicion rather than excitement, but my faith certainly had its role to play. As a Christian I had acquired a powerful image of what it meant to be a human being. I was not sure where this image came from – it was not actively taught as such – but none the less a definite picture developed in my mind, all the more powerful for not being consciously formulated. Lurking in my subconscious it could insidiously destroy me without being confronted for the rubbish that it was.

I thought that a person divided into three parts: body, mind and spirit. I recognized that the parts were all inter-related, but rather as a company chairman was related to managers and managers to the workforce, or, worse still, as a field marshal was related to a lieutenant and a lieutenant to a private in the army. There was a definite pecking order and a hierarchy.

The bottom rung of the hierarchical ladder was the accursed body. The body was perceived as a ravenous and obsessive beast. I thought that if I let my body have its own way I would sleep all night, eat all day and have unwanted pregnancies in between. Bodily desires for food and sleep were intense and strong. They had to be kept under control or they would lead to the sins of the flesh. The body was gross and base. It was acceptable only inasmuch as it was directed by the higher forces of the mind.

The mind was the body's boss. It was an umbrella term covering the brain, the will and the intellect. The mind was respectable; it was the part that made decisions, it juggled with concepts and played with ideas. It was the part of a person encountered if ever she was asked, 'I say, to what extent do you think space and time analogous?' My mind calculated calories in a foreboding manner. When it reached the all-signi-ficant number '1,000' it would say to my body, 'Ha ha! No more.'

But over and above the mind was that lofty and ethereal entity the spirit. I was a little vague as to what the spirit was, but that was precisely because it was sublime. Things of the spirit could never be understood in terms of the mere mind. The spirit was the part of me occupied by the Holy Spirit. It was the part in action when I prayed, the part of which God most approved. For the desires of the spirit were good as surely as the desires of the body (flesh) were bad.

Such was my picture of a human being, and I had a con-sistent picture of holiness. I sinned when I gave in to my body's desires and did not allow them to be directed (ignored, squashed, suppressed) by my spirit. I wanted to be a good Christian. I wanted to be like Jesus. This meant not oversleeping in the morning so there was no time to pray, not getting drunk or having sex – certainly not having sex with myself – and not overeating.

This was very hard, as anyone will know, and it was probably only Christians who have even bothered to try. How was it to be achieved? Well, by gritting my teeth, clenching my fists and *refusing* to give in to my bodily desires. A growth towards God was a growth in willpower. I asked God to give me more.

My church did not enjoy bodies. In the youth group we did not play table tennis or badminton, but prayed and read the Bible together each week. My school did not enjoy bodies. At our girls' private school sport had very low status; the cups and colours were awarded on the last day of term, and it was academic prizes that were received at the high-profile, ceremonious speech day. I did not enjoy my body. I was happy to read but not to swim, to play the piano but not play tennis, to explore my mind but not my clitoris.

I did not respect my body and thought it acceptable only inasmuch as it was governed by the mind or spirit. That is why the idea of retraining myself to eat as my body suggested was so difficult to take on board. It entailed turning upside down what I had believed. It meant ignoring what my mind was telling me and acting as my tummy informed me. It involved listening to the gurgles from within rather than the instructions from the slimming industry without.

But when I radically rethought my faith I realized the idea of spirit resisting the passions of the body simply did not work. It did not work in practice – and I could say that, as a born-again, baptized-in-the-spirit believer – and it did not work in theory either. I realized that I did not divide into three separate parts as I had originally supposed. Even to use the terms 'body', 'mind' and 'spirit' was meaningful only up to a point. When I got in touch with my deepest desires I saw they were neither purely physical nor purely spiritual. My body, mind and spirit were knit together to form the fabric of my being. The desire to hold a person I loved was neither just physical nor just spiritual. It was simply meaningless to talk in such terms.

Furthermore, inasmuch as it was possible to talk of 'bodies' and 'spirits', my faith should have helped me respect the former. For right at the centre of Christianity was none other than a body. It was God's means of revelation. When God chose to redeem the world she did not use an abstract spirit. She did not use an intellectual concept. The word became flesh. Almighty God became a human being – God became a body.

'This is my body', said Jesus to his friends at their last meal together. He did not say 'I leave you my teachings.' He did not say 'Remember what I told you.' Instead he told them to eat his flesh and drink his blood in memory of him. It could be seen as crude, as disgustingly vulgar and physical, as reducing his separation from his Father to an unnecessarily basic level. Or it could be seen as the natural parting gift from the one in whom body and spirit were integrated. It could be a statement of the sheer and utter Godness of our human flesh and blood.

Paul went on to say that the church was Christ's body. He extended the idea of God being embodied in Jesus to that of everyone making up his body on earth. Some were his arms, some his legs, some his eyes. He was illustrating our unity, our indispensability and our continuity with the person of Jesus.

There was so much body business at church. It was central in our celebrations and our understanding of salvation, and yet we never thought about Jesus's body. We totally ignored it. Why did we not think of the body of Christ as in his actual flesh and blood? Why did we not meditate on his hair, his legs, his trunk, his blood, his guts, his sweat? Why did we not imagine those Galilean hills, the hot midday sun, and no deodorants, soap or talc? Did Jesus not have a dripping forehead, sand stuck to his toes, and indigestion? Did God not smell? Did God not need to scratch at times, use a stone when we would use loo paper or wake up in the morning with an erection?

I flinched from the idea as it came into my mind. It seemed irreverent – it seemed disrespectful. Jesus would not have done such things. But why not? If I believed Jesus was beyond having smelly armpits, had I not missed the whole point of the incarnation? Had I not failed to see what it was all about? Surely if 'disrespect' came into it, I was being disrespectful to bodies because I thought of them as base. Surely the irreverence was in perceiving bodies as undignified; surely the word becoming flesh asserted that sweating and hungering and disposing of waste food were not lowly activities. They were thought up by our creator and donned by God himself. How dare we be ashamed of them?

And so I came to understand that bodies were holy. Our bodies that informed us when they needed food, that goose-pimpled and sweated, that curled up and went to sleep were precious and worthy of the utmost respect. God lived in them. Who was I to moan that I had to?

Years after the day when I had looked at my vagina for the first time, I recounted the experience to a friend. She thought it terrible that I found a part of myself disgusting.

'Wherever did such negative feelings come from?', she asked.

'Oh I could never bear watching a rat being dissected in biology either', I tossed off lightly. 'It's all the same sort of stuff.' Mo was not satisfied. She thought a little squeamishness was no excuse for hating yourself. I had to admit that she was right. I decided to have another investigation. My equipment was the same, my justification different. I was not doing it to insert a tampon, I was doing it for its own sake. I was doing it because my body was good.

There is a pleasure in receiving a gift and unwrapping it to disclose what is already yours. There is an incredulous joy in opening your legs to discover something that is already yourself. So there was my clitoris, my urethra, my vagina. It was incredible to think I had never looked at them before and yet they had always been there. My urethra was so tiny. To think that I had imagined I could get a tampon up it! But it was my vagina that I found the most amazing.

I contracted and dilated the muscles, imagining that I was giving birth. I watched it open and close like the mouth of a goldfish taking a slow feed. I did not know that I could do that. What a fascinating mechanism! But it was more than some alien clinical apparatus necessary for procreation. That dilating hole was mine – no, it was me. I used my vagina as an aid to prayer.

79

First of all I thought of what my vagina was for. It was for sex and a doorway to my womb. I imagined having a period pain and placed my hand on the corresponding place on my tummy. That must be where my womb was, right in the middle of me. I imagined the passage from my vagina to my centre and meditated on another person coming inside me, the journey of the sperm, swimming up the uterus to fertilize the egg. I thought of a new person living inside my body. How could I ever have imagined that without a sense of wonder? Would that little being actually live inside me? Breathing the air that I breathe, eating the food that I eat, joined to me by a cord, her home my womb?

Heavenly Mother, how I would work to share with you in the work of your creation. How I would pant, how I would toil, how I would scream in labour so that the person who had lived inside me could live out in the world. I imagined a dark head emerging from me and the sound of our child's cry. Give her to me, bring her here. I want her in my arms. Wash her? What from? That blood has been her home. Cut her from me? Not yet, just put her on my breast. I want her to hear the beating of my heart, to feel the warmth of my exhausted body. For in my body, my breasts, there will be all that she needs to nourish her in her first few months of living. My milk will sustain her. My skin against her skin, her body against my body, my body that has given her life.

I had despised my body. I had thought of it as less than spiritual and beneath the one who made it, God. I had resented it every month as it had filled with fluid and caused me pain – small price to pay for being able to give birth. I had thought my body base, my labia disgusting. I had thought that suppression of my bodily desires was the means to holiness and God.

I did that meditation one Sunday morning before church. As I received communion I offered my vagina, my body and my all to God. He had given his body, I gave mine. As I ate the bread I imagined digesting it until it quite literally, physically became a part of me. What more could Jesus have done to assure us that bodies are good? I heard the words as for the first time, 'Offer your souls and bodies as a living sacrifice.'

As I became glad to be a body I began to enjoy physical activity. For years I had been too self-conscious to go swimming, believing I was fat. My healing involved learning to celebrate my body by jumping into the swimming pool each day. I would feel the water whoosh and champagne-bubble around me. I would snort it from my nose, shake it from my face and breaststroke up and down until exhausted. Familiar legs glided mysteriously past in the silent underwater world. Lying on my back, resting in the cradling buoyancy, I heard the lap, lap, splash echo in the hollow shell of the indoor pool. I returned home relaxed, hungry, and glad to be flesh, bones and blood.

In learning to honour my body, as in the other aspects of my healing, friends were indispensable. One night Steve came to see me. We sat cross-legged on the floor and talked into the timeless hours of the night. Then he decided to hold me.

I curled up into a ball as he pulled me on to his legs, wrapped me up with his arms and rested his head sideways on top of mine. Having ensured that I was enveloped he held me firmly and gently without stroking, kissing or squeezing me. We were totally still. All I could feel was him breathing and the beating of his heart.

As he held me my tears gradually rose from deeper and deeper places. Through his solid, engulfing touch he was communicating an acceptance of my body that I knew I had to learn to sense for myself. I realized that I was not some spirit that just happened to be passing through an unfortunate body, but I was my body, all the way through, from my heartbeat right out to the skin which Steve touched.

What if God had made me anything less than a body? I had tried to be more spiritual than I had been made. I had indulged in a super-spirituality more sick than a heathen's happy hedonism. I had imagined that my holy body that sweated for me when I was hot, was sick when I ate bad food, goose-pimpled when I was cold and cuddled the people I loved could not inform me when it needed food.

Gradually I had the faith to listen to my appetite.

Believing in the incarnation meant believing in being a body. I trusted that my stomach would inform me when I was hungry and when I had had enough to eat. I was graced with the courage to try. It took months of careful practice to undo my four compulsive years.

Whenever I felt the desire to dive mouth first into the bread bin, set up igloo in the fridge or buy out the corner sweet shop, I had to ask myself 'Am I hungry?' 'Am I hungry?', I asked as I reached for the seconds of ice cream; 'Am I hungry?', as I lay in bed fantasizing about food; 'Am I hungry?', as I headed for the larder as soon as I entered the house.

The listening did not stop there. If I decided that yes, it was hunger that I was experiencing, then the exercise had to continue. 'Now then, what kind of hungry am I? Is this a fish-and-chips-eaten-in-the-newspaper-made-soggy-with-vinegar kind of hungry? Is it a fresh-crispy-salad-with-soft-cottage-cheese-and-a-newly-baked-granary-roll kind of want? Is it a Marmite-and-marmalade-on-toast kind of desire, or simply a dunking-digestive-biscuits-in-a-cup-of-tea kind of feeling?' I would sit and listen to my hunger and once I had decided what I wanted I ate it. You ate whatever you wanted? I ate whatever I wanted. If I wanted a Knickerbocker Glory I would eat that. If I wanted dolcelatte cheese on Ryvita with sliced tomato sprinkled with salt and pepper I would eat that. If I wanted fresh pasta with a rich bolognese sauce topped with grated parmesan cheese I would eat that, and if halfway through I decided I was full, I would stop eating whatever just-what-I-felt-like I had chosen.

It was not easy. I had spent so long ignoring my body's messages that I did not grow in touch with them without making mistakes. At first when I genuinely did not know if I was hungry or not I would always give myself the benefit of the doubt. I supposed that I needed half a loaf of bread when in fact three slices would have been sufficient. Out of habit I would consume half a packet of biscuits before I had even thought about it. I believed that I should eat what I wanted to eat, but discerning what I wanted took practice.

It also took time.

'Do you want an orange?', a friend asked as we finished our meal.

'Um, wait a minute. I'm not sure', I replied. I shut my eyes, put my hands on my stomach and concentrated. 'Eat it, eat it. Do I want to eat it?', I asked my insides. The orange became heavy in my friend's hand. 'No, I don't think I do, but I may be wrong', I concluded. We both laughed.

And so I relearnt how to eat. It was a long, slow process. At first I put on weight. I had given up my between-binge fasts but I was still misinterpreting my body's messages. Extra pounds displayed themselves on my legs and tummy. But as I grew in touch with myself a most surprising thing happened. I discovered that my body was reliable – my body knew best. When I ate exactly what I wanted to eat I did not become fatter. In fact, so slowly that I did not notice, my weight dropped off. When I stopped fighting my appetite and honoured it instead, it did its job. When I elevated my body to its God-given place, it showed me how to eat and made me whole.

7

Projections on the body

I did not want to go out that night. I felt fat. I was to meet up with seven friends in town and go on to a concert, but I did not want to go because I was fat. Penny should have been here half an hour ago. She was not coming to the concert herself but she had the tickets for me to give to the others. If I did not go to the concert then the tickets did not go, and if the tickets did not go then no one went.

I looked in the mirror and prayed that Penny would arrive too late. I was fat. I stared in disgust at the spreading hips, recoiled at the full thighs and sneered at the enormous breasts. I winced as I considered that everyone who set eyes on me would be staring, recoiling and sneering too. I could not go out. I could not do it. 'Please God, may Penny arrive too late with the tickets. Or may she lose them. Or may she fall off her bike and knock herself unconscious . . .'

'Penny, how lovely to see you.' I opened the door in response to the knock. Penny waltzed in, thin. It would be so lovely to be as thin as her. (God, why didn't you knock her unconscious?)

'I've got the tickets,' said Penny, producing the death

warrants. I must have pouted because she went on to ask, 'Is anything wrong?'

'Oh, Pen', I said, responding to her gentleness, 'I really don't want to go out tonight.'

'Why not?' she inquired in the same inviting manner. She was being as kind as possible, but I felt irritated. What did she mean 'Why not?' How typical of a thin person. It was obvious why not. Did she really have to ask?

'Because,' I said slowly, inhaling painfully, 'because', I said, 'I'm fat.'

'What?' said Penny. She was obviously surprised. 'You're not fat.' They all said that. All my friends said the same, but it was not what I wanted to hear. Well it was, yes, in a way it was, but in another way I felt that they were being cruel in try-ing to lure me into a false sense of security by their well-meaning dishonesty. Some of them lied to me, even saying that I was beautiful.

'You're beautiful', said Penny. 'Everybody thinks so.'

'Well I don't feel beautiful.' I was sulking now. 'How I feel' – I closed my eyes trying to describe the feeling accurately – 'is fat and as though nobody likes me.'

'Oh, Jo', and Penny looked troubled as she said it quietly. 'I'm sorry that I don't understand. I wish I did, but I don't. I just don't understand how you of all people think that people don't like you. Wherever you go you leave your Joey mark. Every-one that meets you loves you. If people don't like you then how do you explain the constant stream of people in your room at all hours of the day and night?'

I could not deny the existence of this stream, especially as I had moaned to Penny earlier about how it meant that I could never seem to get any work done. However, I had my own way of interpreting it.

'It's because', I said genuinely believing it at the time, 'they all feel sorry for me.'

'What?' Penny was running out of patience now. 'And why should anyone feel sorry for YOU?' I was running out of patience too. I had told her, hadn't I?

'Because I'm FAT.'

'Oh sorry, I forgot.' Penny and I sat on the bed in silence. She looked at her watch. 'Look, I've got to go and you've got to go.' A look of doubt flashed across her face. 'You will go, won't you?'

'Yeah, I'll go', I said sulkily.

'Good.' Penny stood up to leave. She looked me in the eye. 'I am sorry that I don't understand, Jo.'

'That's OK, Pen. See you.' I saw Penny out. A head appeared round the door.

'You're not fat', it said, and disappeared.

What I wanted more than anything else was food. I felt fat. I needed to diet. What had I got in the house? I rushed downstairs and rummaged through some tins. I had only just had my supper. 'Am I hungry, am I hungry?', I managed to ask myself just as the bread was about to find its way in. 'Am I really hungry?', I said as I put the bread down. 'If you are hungry you can eat this. That is a promise, but perhaps you stand more chance of finding out up in your room rather than down in the kitchen.' I went upstairs and consulted my tummy.

I was not hungry. I had had lentil loaf for tea and I could feel it warm and stodgy in my stomach. In fact I was very full, but I still had an insatiable desire to eat. Physically I was well satisfied but emotionally I required sustenance. My stomach was full up but my heart was empty. Remembering the bread, I stood up and made for the door, but I just about managed to sit down again, promising myself that if I really wanted the loaf I could have it soon.

'Right, so you are not hungry. Well, how are you feeling?', I asked myself. I was full, so why did I feel the desire to stuff my face? I knew I was not obese, so why did I think I was? I knew that if I lost a stone nothing else in my life would change. Where was the abracadabra in going on a diet? If I was not hungry but still wanted to eat, what confusion had arisen inside?

I sat still, closed my eyes and listened to the feelings raging within. 'I want to eat. I want the bread. Give it to me. Give it to me. I'm fat. I'm grotesque. Yuk. Aaaaagh. I'm revolting.

Food. Diet. Diet. Lose four stone. Panic. Flab. Aaaaaaaaagh!' I allowed the feelings to surface and make themselves known. Then slowly I told my insides, 'Jo, diets don't work. Penny has just told you you are beautiful. What are you trying to cover up by cramming yourself even fuller?' I replied, 'HELP! I CAN'T COPE. HELP! I'M FRIGHTENED. I DON'T WANT TO GO OUT. HELP! HELP! S.O.S.'

I took my time and gradually worked out what I was frightened of. Friends from two different circles were coming together in the seven people that were going to the concert. Half of them were socialist, feminist, bean-eating humanists, jazzing their trousers, dangling their earrings, their heads full of social concern and the limited nature of the world's resources. The other half were fundamentalist, Bible-based, Evangelical Christians, One-Waying their sweatshirts, Jesusing their sandals, their heads full of Bible verses and the unlimited nature of the Kingdom's supernatural powers. These two groups of people were likely to clash when we went out for a beer/orange juice afterwards.

So part of my problem was doubting my resources of tact and the ability to steer the conversation away from any controversial issues. I did not like to imagine the scenario when a woman about to explore becoming a lesbian was told that homosexuals ought to be stoned because it said so in the Bible. But the problem was deeper than that. These two irreconcilable people represented two irreconcilable parts of me. I had been a socialist feminist with my socialist feminist friends and an Evangelical Christian with my Evangelical Christian friends. I was still struggling to work out how to get these parts of me together. I could not cope with them meeting face to face in armed combat.

'So, how are you feeling?', I asked myself as I prayed. 'I'm afraid. I'm nervous. I'm confused about who I am and who God is. I'm worried my friends won't like me if they don't get on. I don't want any aggro. I wish I could find a Jo hat rather than wearing a feminist hat for some people and a Christian one for others.'

The dialogue within me continued. 'That's OK. Feel the

fear. Feel nervous. Feel disliked. Feel two-faced. It's not that bad, is it?' 'No.' 'Are you hungry?' 'No.' 'Would eating bread help?' 'No.' 'Would being thin make any difference?' 'No.' 'Well done, Jo. Well done, God in Jo.' I stayed with my feelings until the panic had subsided. Then I picked up my bicycle lights and left the house.

Getting in touch with my appetite was one thing, experiencing my feelings was another. It was all very well listening to see if I was hungry, but I often discovered I was not and yet still had a compulsion to eat. 'Am I hungry?', I would ask, and if I was I would eat until I was satisfied. If I was not it was more complicated. I had to get in touch with my feelings.

I needed to investigate this common phenomenon. If I was not hungry then why was I feeling the desire for chocolate? What was my compulsive behaviour doing for me? Why was I obsessed? What was I doing when I made my midnight journeys to the kitchen? What was actually going on inside besides the digestion of a whole packet of cereal?

As I practised asking myself this question I recognized that my eating disorder was serving a purpose for me. It was protecting me from pain. I was a compulsive eater because I could not cope with my problems. I could not bear the fear, the suffering, the loneliness that life brings. When I responded to all I saw around me it was more than I could take, so I developed a mechanism of cutting myself off from my feelings. I created an eating disorder so I never had to face the other pains of living.

I became a compulsive eater at around the age of fifteen or sixteen. It was a time when I began to feel a pain and an aloneness that I had not experienced before. I had to decide what I wanted to do with my life and for the first time make decisions of significance. I was forced, in short, to ask what I valued and what I made of this being alive business. I tried to look life and myself straight in the eye. I took it all seriously.

Life is short, I would muse, and perhaps the most important thing is to make life as long as possible. So I considered becoming a doctor. But what's the use of being a doctor if we all get blown up in a nuclear war, I reasoned. I would decide that being a politician was what really counted. But then how can you work for world peace if you had not discovered peace within, I queried, and I would fantasize about living in a hippy commune, swinging my beads and settling into flower power. Those were the kinds of questions I was asking myself, and I was feeling increasingly alone.

I felt alone because in a sense we are. Having to make decisions made me aware of that. In the last analysis it was only me that could live my life. I could listen to others and ask their opinions but it was for me to weigh up their advice, and to decide whether to heed it or whether to rebel. I was alone and that was that. No one else could be me for me. In my brighter moments I found that thought exciting and exhilarating; in my darker moments I felt afraid and aware of an emptiness that no other person could fill.

I was also becoming aware of the immense amount of suffering in the world. As I looked beyond my immediate environment I could not be blind to pain. I made friends with Alan, who was the same age as me. He had no arms. I got to know some of the lads who roamed the city centre in gangs. Their bodies were scarred and bruised from fights, their hearts were hard and they were fearful of going out unprotected. I started to read about the millions of people who had no food and wondered by what fluke I came to be a woman who would not have to watch her children starve and die. It was beginning to penetrate my consciousness that the world was not a cosy place.

We all grow up sometime. We all reach a point when we realize that the food does not just appear on the table, and that there are people less fortunate than ourselves, and that we have choice and choice entails responsibility. We suffer; we see others suffer; we know that we will die. The feelings that this awareness evokes are never comfortable, but in my case they were intensified by my parents' sudden separation and divorce. One day they seemed to be happily married; the next it was clear they were not. One day I was chugging along, life as normal; then my world crumbled into pieces around me. The loving relationship from which I had grown was translated into legal terms and grounds for separation. We moved to a different house, both my parents were in acute pain and we did not know where the money was coming from.

'The world is not a cosy place', whispered the Ethiopian woman as I turned the television off and started cooking the supper. 'The world is not a cosy place', whispered the prostitute on the street corner as I hurried past purposefully before I too was asked my price. 'The world is not a cosy place', the fact of my parents' divorce blasted in my ear with a force and a vivacity that I could not ignore, could not suppress and could not escape from.

The world was not a cosy place and there was nothing I could do to make it cosy. Nothing. I could earn a comfortable living, get a car and a mortgage; I could marry and have three bright and healthy children. But all I could do was postpone the moments of pain, disease and death. I could not evade suffering. Suffering was.

I began to live on a different level. My guts were crying out. My peers were concerned with going on the pill and passing their A levels; I was concerned about poverty and injustice and the way communication between human beings can break down and what they have created together can be destroyed.

What do you do when you are seventeen years of age, experiencing feelings the like of which you have never experienced before? What do you do when you are living at a depth and intensity that isolates you from those around you? What do you do when you want to get your A levels so you can go to university and get a good job and meet a nice man, but you are feeling in such pain that when you should be learning your trigonometric equations you are lying on your back, clasping your stomach and crying out, 'Ow, ow, ow'?

Do you continue to live from the depths of that pain? Do you carry on experiencing it day in and day out, or do you cut yourself off from it? Do you make yourself a blanket and wrap it round you so you can no longer see, touch, feel the raw horribleness of the world?

We all find ways of cutting ourselves off from pain. Some people turn to drugs, some people use sex. Some people fall in love and then fall in love again and again with less than a week in between each most wonderful person they have ever met in their life. Some people go to religious meetings and sing happy choruses and deceive themselves that horrible things like that never happen to nice people who follow Jesus. I became a compulsive eater.

Compulsive eating was an anaesthetic, a way of growing numb. It was a way of creating an alternative problem so I never had to face the bigger ones. Compulsive eating enabled me to lose touch with my feelings. It cut me off from my deepest pains. 'I feel fat', I said to Penny, and I believed that was the size of it. It was the safest emotion to feel.

My compulsive eating was a sophisticated mechanism evolved to cut me off from my feelings. It worked in three ways. The first way was the actual act of eating itself. It was a readily available means of feeling nothing. I shovelled one mouthful in before I had finished the last. All I could see was the cream cake – the outside world did not exist. It was more like masturbating than anything else, but it was even easier. For however long the binge lasted, be it three minutes, ten minutes or twenty, I had some temporary relief from the world within me.

The second way was in what I experienced after I had eaten. For once a binge was over I would experience an alternative feeling to my pain. I would feel full up – full up and hungry maybe, but overwhelmingly full up. It was that after-Christmas-dinner feeling when you are too full to go for a walk, play Monopoly or even open the rest of the presents. You sit on the sofa like the Christmas pudding itself, stuck, oozing brandy and heavy sickliness. But I did not feel like that just at Christmas – I felt it almost every day for four years. If I broke my diet in the morning I would continue to feel puddinged for the rest of the day. As soon as there was space for a little more food a lot more was shovelled in. It seemed I was not comfortable unless I was uncomfortable. I had to feel full. Full up of food, there was no room for 'angry', 'hurt', 'frightened', 'nervous' – just 'full up' instead.

The third way was more complicated. To understand how it worked it is necessary to get inside my compulsively eating world. If I was not actually anaesthetizing myself from feeling by the act of eating, or if I was not feeling full up instead of pain and fear, then I was feeling 'I will start my diet tomorrow.' Really being alive would happen the next day. That protected me from experiencing the day I was in.

I was obsessed. Everything I saw, I saw through the eyes of fat and thin. I could not meet a friend without wondering what it would be like to look like her. I could not go to sleep at night without imagining my food turning into tummy. I could not wake up in the morning without resolving to go on a diet that day. I could not sit in a lecture/ache in aerobics/get holy in prayer meetings/jostle at the bar without thinking of figures and food.

I was fat and wanted to be thin. That would be when the real Jo came alive. All I experienced now was but a fat way to a thin end. Fat Jo did not wear imaginative clothes, fat Jo did not play squash with the others, fat Jo did not stand a chance with the super studs. But when Jo was thin she would. Life would begin again.

When I was thin, I fantasized, all sorts of things would happen. I would not retain the same basic shape only thinner; everything else would change as well. My frame, which is large, would become petite. My hips, which are wide, would become narrow and neat. My hair, which is short and spiky, would undulate down my shoulders in thick, dark, abundant curls. My overgrown baby hands would develop elegant, nail-varnished fingers. My white, pale skin would become a tropical everbrown. The spots which appear monthly would be squeezed into clear complexion eternal, and stretchmarks, body hair, perspiration and foot odour would vanish mysteriously from my existence.

But it did not stop there. In my world of thin and fantasy the magic worked in other ways. Once I weighed eight stone, zero pounds, not only would I stand at the door of the party stunning every guest with my beautiful body, but I would hold them spellbound by the wit and charm of my powerful personality. When I became Media Woman herself I would slip into a slick suit, nonchalantly shrugging off my latest promotion. As

Ms Cosmopolitan I would slide out of old relationships and glide into new ones, my only problem being which to choose from my long list of suitors. When I was thin the world would work my way. There would be no struggle, no pain.

This was my obsessive world of compulsive eating. It was a world of fat and thin. The struggles were fat, the ease was thin. The unrequited love, the drizzly Monday morning and the grey dreariness of the factories and urine-smelling tower blocks were fat. The glamour, the prestige, the holidays in Barbados were thin – and I was starting my diet tomorrow.

If the clothes in the cheap fashion boutiques did not fit it was because I was fat – there was some logic in that. If I fancied him but he did not fancy me it was because of my figure – it never occurred to me to look for an alternative explanation. Sitting in the launderette on a wet Wednesday evening, making myself dizzy as I watched the washing go round, I would resolve to go on a diet tomorrow. The formidable line of files in the careers office and the threatening white glare of the job application form would evoke in me yearnings to be thin. Queuing up to sign on amongst dirty, depressed and impoverished people I would curse myself for being overweight. Receiving a bank statement and realizing I had run out of money before I had run out of month was enough to get me calorie counting.

It was so reassuring to start my diet tomorrow. It protected me by fostering the illusion that pain is avoidable. By translating every situation into fat and thin I could deceive myself that the trouble-free life was only two stone away. Every time I said, 'If only I was thin . . .', I distanced myself from the pain I could not afford to feel.

It took me a long time to work out that this was an element of my compulsive eating and even longer to work it through. I could see that it was not rational. Contrary to what all the advertisers would have me believe, I knew life would not become aftershave-scented and microwave-blessed at eight stone, zero pounds. I resisted the lies with my mind but I swallowed them emotionally – and the rest of the larder too. After all, it was my heart my compulsion was trying to protect.

Once again, it was in listening to other people that I became

93

whole. It was friends telling me their problems and my desire to feel for them that freed me to feel for myself. When I was compulsive and obsessed I could never believe that thin people really experienced pain. Fiona might have been upset about her boyfriend but she was slim enough to catch another one; Anne might have been feeling guilty and worried about her work but at least she did not need to go on a diet; Julie might have been distressed because her father was seriously ill but, well, she was thin.

One night I had a startling thought. Liz was describing how her mother had died. She talked of the frequent journeys to the hospital and watching her being in more and more intense pain. She recounted how her mother had held her for the last time despite the physical suffering that touching caused her. She explained how they had discussed the care for her nine-year-old brother and how she had returned home to tell him that Mummy was dead. I wept. I wanted to feel the whole agony with her but I was inhibited because she was thin.

'Stop it, Jo. Stop it', I rebuked myself on reflection. 'Was it any consolation to Liz that she was thin? Did Joy's slimness help her when she had a still-born child? Did Tonia's skinniness prevent her from attempting suicide? How dare you distance yourself from their pain with your lies? How dare you cheapen their suffering by translating it into fat and thin?'

'How many of these thin women do you need to know?', I told myself in a moment as frightening as it was liberating. 'Just how many more thin women do you have to hold, weep with, live with, suffer with before it breaks through into your obsessively protected heart that even being thin does not take away the deep pains of living?'

As a compulsive eater I had lost touch with my appetite. But I had also lost touch with my feelings. Rather than experience the darkness and the agony of life, or for that matter its light and ecstasy, I would simply feel fat. I learnt to retrace my appetite by asking myself, 'Am I hungry?' and then eating whatever I wanted. I learnt to retrace my feelings by giving myself space to experience them whenever I felt the urge to smother them in doughnuts.

'Am I hungry? No. So why do I want to eat? Am I worried? Am I afraid? Am I guilty? What's going on in this life of mine? Is my heart hurting? What are my guts groaning? God, you are in me. What are you saying?'

As an Evangelical Christian I had pictured God as 'up there'. I had imagined him shining in splendour from his lofty throne while the angels wafted round saying 'Yes my Lord'. I had thought of him up in the sky with millions of telephones, answering them in rotation if we should give him a call. I prayed to someone outside and invited him in. But Jesus said that the kingdom of God is not over here or over there but within us. He himself was called Emmanuel, meaning 'God with us'. In Jesus, God was revealing the way of becoming more divine in the way of becoming more human. He was showing that where we find God is in our insides.

That means that prayer was not about cupping my hands around my mouth and bellowing 'Oi! Can you hear me?' to the sky. It was not about trying to get through to some distant being despite the ceiling and the clouds that stand in the way. It was about listening to myself. It was allowing God-in-me to make herself known. It was giving space to my deepest place, the seat of my passions, and letting them permeate the rest of our being.

Our Heavenly Mother was not distant from her creation. She was not aloof, observing events in a detached uninterested manner. She was shaking in every junkie that comes down, starving in every child that has no food, shivering in the homeless, weeping in the bereaved, singing at the party, laughing at the banana skin, and ecstatic in every baby conceived into life. She was present in every moment and in each person. She invited us to respond to her, to live with all that we are. She called us to shake, to starve, to shiver, to weep, to sing, to laugh, to be in ecstasy with her.

And so when I was a compulsive eater it was not just my pain that I was cutting off from, it was God-in-me too. In refusing to listen to my deepest parts I was ignoring God. My compulsive obsession was the antithesis of prayer. It was saying 'Sshh sshh sshh' to the feelings inside rather than 'Ow ow ow' with the one who invites us to share them with her. God was crying out in my guts and I did not want to listen.

But the other side of that was that learning how to eat was growing in touch with God. 'Am I hungry?' was the first step of my prayer journey. If I was then I would eat. If I was not then I would give myself time to feel whatever I was suppressing. The desire to binge became very creative. It was my chance to know the world around and within me. It was exciting, it was exhilarating, and it hurt. I was no longer living in the fantasy world of starting my diet tomorrow; I was not living at one step removed. The blanket I had wrapped around myself was slowly being taken away. There was the world and there was me and there was nothing in between. I was naked. I was raw. I was more fully alive.

If being alive hurt, then being more fully alive hurt even more. Being a compulsive eater was painful, but so was not being one. The choice between the way of compulsion and the way of prayer was not between pain and the absence of pain. It was the choice between the pain of being destroyed or the pain of being redeemed.

I learnt to choose the pain of prayer rather than the pain of an eating disorder. I learnt to choose the pain of feeling with God rather than the pain of cutting myself off from her – I tried to stay awake in Gethsemane rather than fall asleep. I preferred truth to lies. I risked allowing God-in-me to be.

8

The resurrection of the body

'BEFORE YOU READ THIS MAKE SURE THERE IS SOME-ONE WITH YOU.' I left the supper party immediately so that I could be alone. The words were a preface to a letter from my mother; I had had other letters of this kind before. It was how my mum heralded her tidings of bad news, and though I did not heed her advice I was grateful for the warning. After all, at the time I was not thinking about the irony of my reacting to her advice by ignoring it; my energy was absorbed in preparing for a shock.

I was in Cairo at the time. Liz, my flatmate, and I had been going through a difficult patch in our lives. 'What we need', said Liz, in a moment of spontaneity, 'is a holiday. Let's travel through Europe by land and then fly on to Cairo.' It was decided in a moment – we wanted to go. Liz gave up her job, I took a month off work. We took our savings out of the bank (and more), put our rucksacks on our backs and hitchhiked away from our problems . . . or so we thought.

As I made my way to the balcony I wondered who had died. My gran had just died, so at least it was not her. My mum was recovering from cancer. What if it was her who had died? But no, silly, she had written the letter. It could not be her that was dead. Perhaps she was writing to say that the doctors had found another lump and I had better hurry home in case she died soon. I opened the letter. It was not about my mum; it was about a dear friend of the family, Dave, dear, twenty-one-year-old Dave. Dave, who had been so helpful at my sister's wedding; Dave, who had been there at my brother's twenty-first; Dave, who had grown from greasy hair to spiky hair, from pre-pubescent insecurities to a deep belief in his own worth.

I imagined Dave at polytechnic finishing his exams, looking forward to the time when they would all be over. I imagined him putting down his pen after his last essay and thinking of the weekend he was to enjoy at home. I imagined him getting into a car with his friends and sitting in the luggage compartment because there was not enough room in the front. I saw the car spinning along out of control, the back flap flying open, Dave flying out, banging his head against a wall and lying there, dead.

'Tragic' as a word was the best that we had, but I did not find it good enough. It did not effectively convey the futility of the event or the meaninglessness of the situation. How could it be that human life was so vulnerable? It was one slight error of judgement that caused the car to turn. How disproportionate a consequence – what a senseless scenario. What kind of a being thought up a universe with causes and effects like that? Was God a tyrant or was he a sadist or was God an Almighty Dumb-wit?

Talking of God, or rather wailing of him, the people of Cairo were being called to prayer. The wail coming from the top of the Citadel was an evocation to worship God at the mosque. In the context of Muslim culture it sounded just as beautiful as the clanging of church bells does to Christians. The men were responding in obedience. Women were not allowed in the mosque at this time. An array of kaftans left their homes and made their way for prayer.

'Stop', I wanted to cry from my view on the balcony. 'Don't do it. Come back', to the kaftans below. 'How can you kneel to the East in honour of Allah? How can you senselessly believe that God is good? Look around you. Can you see?

Either God is impotent, in which case he is not God, or the universe is ruled by a bloody-minded sadist.'

That afternoon we had been to the City of the Dead, a suburb of Cairo. We had chattered merrily in the taxi, jumped out, crossed the road (no mean achievement) and confronted a sight we had never seen before.

This was poverty, the real stuff, the kind you find on posters in Oxfam shops or described by organizations like Cafod or Christian Aid. 'Mumpkin ellum' (or something like that), said Poverty, tugging at my trouser leg. 'Mumpkin ellum', he said, meaning 'May I have a pen?' He was knee-high, with black eyes and a grubby brown face wearing a simple pyjama outfit. He did not have any shoes. The coveted 'ellum' was a ballpoint pen, the cheap and nasty kind you use to write a cheque in the supermarket and then forget to pick up because you are busy with your shopping – the sort you always lose before the ink runs out. Looking into his eyes I wanted to oblige, but his brothers and sisters had begun to 'mumpkin ellum' too. A score of little fists were tugging at our trousers. As pied pipers, we smiled and waded our way through.

I had found it easy to get romantic about people dying of poverty. I would look at glossy photographs of them by charitable organizations and think how endearing the children were. The problem with pictures is that they appeal only to the sense of sight, and I was rather lazy at using my imagination. I saw a fly on a child's face which I supposed would go away; I did not realize that flies were everywhere all the time. I could not hear the relentless roaring of the traffic on the over-crowded roads or the constant blasting of horns. Nor could I feel the weight of the hot, oppressive air which makes even being outside claustrophobic. I had not realized that any colour in life fades as everything is besmirched with a layer of dirt. There is nothing romantic in never quite knowing if you are going to be sick or not.

Some women were standing at the door of their home. They smiled, we smiled, they gestured to us to go in. We kept smiling and nodding to each other as signs of friendship and assurance. There was no way we could refuse the dirty cup of tea. The room was not much larger than the double bed that was in it. There was a fridge, a television and some clothes hung on the wall. This was the home of one family; the other woman's family lived in the room above. The animals lived on the roof on top of that. The chickens had a run, the human beings did not. I had not thought that overcrowding was a problem, not in hot countries where you could always go outside. I did not realize that the streets of the maze are so narrow that two people cannot walk down side by side. I had not realized that boxes full of people were stacked on top of each other and beside each other and in front of and behind each other in all directions for miles around. It is hard to imagine never, ever having the train fare to get out of the city for a sense of space.

'Suffering', I was told, 'is a result of human sin. We bring it upon ourselves because we disobey God.' For years I had believed it, or pretended to believe it, so that I would fulfil the entry requirements for heaven. Sitting on a balcony in Cairo with Dave dead, I could not accept that it was true. Only a Cosmic Sadist could ask his creation to believe such bunkum.

'I actually do not believe in the death penalty, Lord', I prayed. 'I believe in the sanctity of human life. I believe, Lord, that even a mass murderer has the right to life. These, Lord, are my values and the values of our society too. It is a shame, God Almighty, that these values are not yours.

'Even if it is all our fault – Cairo, David, the lot – why can you not do something about it, if you are God? Or if you could foresee the consequences of giving us free will, why not abandon your plans for a universe? Would it not have been better to stick with God the Son and God the Spirit, rather than allow this mess of a world to come into existence? It seems, with all due respect, Lord, that at the end of the day, we have no choice but to "choose" to be bumped off, any way. And God, if you were sorry, I might be able to accept it. I could respond to an apology but not a "worship me" command. Besides, I cannot pander to your egotism. It is probably the root of your sadism.'

When I was in Egypt I bought an alabaster jar. I bought it

for my sister and her husband as a wedding present. They had got married the year before and I had been searching for a special present ever since. I did not want to buy them something Habitat-trendy or Russell-Hobbes-gadgety. At last I found an alabaster jar.

The jar was special in many different ways. Alabaster was a beautiful stone – it was soft with interesting lines in it; it invited you to touch it, to feel the grain. The jar was plain, just round with a rim. It had a perfection in its simplicity. It was not highly polished as a vulgar marble would be. It displayed the natural features of the stone.

When we were cycling through the Valley of Kings, Liz's purse had dropped out of her pocket. A little boy had cried 'Stop!', and picked it up for her. He then invited us in for food and a drink. We had not eaten that day, because we could not find food. The Egyptian family displayed a generosity quite alien to the British, and it was this family that had made the alabaster jar. Buying it from them was a sign of gratitude to them. I hoped that in my sister's home it would be a source of happy memories too.

The purchase was costly and so too was the care of it. The alabaster jar became my personal Egyptian mummy. Every morning when we began a journey I would cram it full of underwear. I would wrap it round with my sheet sleeping bag and towel and put it in my rucksack. The rest of the packing was arranged around it. At night I would un-mummify my jar, feel its texture, admire its shape and find it a safe place for the night. I performed this ritual every morning and night until we caught the plane home and landed safely in England.

England – we knew we were home. We knew we were home with the first breath of the fresh London air, when the pavements seemed so clean we could have knelt down and licked them, when we were free to be sexually daring and provocative by exposing our bare elbows to any who wished to look. What else makes home home? It is finding the front door is blocked by a month's supply of post. It is the simple pleasures, like having an abundance of that useful stuff that hangs on a roll in a little room. It is giving away your presents, like my alabaster jar.

I eagerly unpacked my rucksack to recover my mummy,

glad that this would be for the last time. I was in no way surprised by what I saw. I was not even disappointed. I found shells of alabaster that once had been a jar.

I was not surprised because life was like that, so it seemed. I had had my suspicions, but now I knew. Dave's death had confirmed that in my mind. We toil, we struggle and we hope to make life good, but we are always defeated and we cannot hope to win. Ultimately we come to nothing, we are destroyed and so we die. It had happened to Dave, it had happened to my jar, it would certainly happen to us all. Life is futile. It is simple as that.

Depression seemed the only appropriate response to life – that and anger at the God who had given it to us. I went to work because I had to, and did very little else.

Every so often I would tell God what I thought of him. Many would have thought my prayers were blasphemous. I was being honest with God – but I was praying. Gone were the days when I could not afford to feel; behind me was the temptation to smother pain with cream cakes. I was going to experience the world no longer in the black and white of compulsion, but in the technicolour of truth. I allowed all that was in me to respond to what I touched around me. I let God-in-me be.

The depression lingered. In the suffocating darkness there was always the temptation to run away from gruesome reality. A part of me wanted to shut out the fact that Dave had died. It wanted to hide it in the recesses of my mind and pretend it had never happened. It wanted to eat and return to the security of my fat and thin world. But I was determined not to do this.

Yes, I probably could forget Dave or at least get to a point where the circumstances of his death no longer filled me with such horror. I could grow numb to it, become immune to it and pretend I had got over it. I could deceive myself and live a lie. For death was death, and death, in a manner of speaking, was an unavoidable fact of life. For this reason I had to confront it. I had to come to terms with a life that ended in death, and if that was impossible then depressed I would remain.

I went for a walk by the river. It was a summer evening – in fact it was almost night. Warm red blotches were permeating from the fireball that was rolling down the sky, unable to contain itself. The last man was walking home. His dog was laughing beside him, trotting along with his tongue hanging out. With a buzz and a whirl the last fisherman wound up his rod and silhouetted away. The last mower was humming on the lawn, the last boat was rippling by. The river was still, the sun was set and there was peace.

Tenderness was making itself known from somewhere deep inside. It had not quite been extinguished in the smothering depression. I sat there, very still, and imbibed the beauty of the evening, and I let tenderness be. And from tenderness, very gently, very softly, God-in-me became. I rolled over, lay on my stomach and wept.

Somewhere, beneath all the shock and anger, was the recognition that God was not macho. He was not all-glorious above without being all-suffering below. He was not a mighty king sitting back complacently on his soft, cushioned throne, exhaling slowly from his fat cigar, preparing a small thunderbolt on account of my two fingertips which I had thrust for his sake heavenwards.

God was Jesus who wept when Lazarus died. God was Jesus who sweated drops of blood. God was Jesus who ached and suffered and bled and died. God was not so much sorry as stuck right in there, starving to death in Cairo, dying in Dave, smashed in the jar. It was not a matter of God versus us or vice versa. It was God in us – God in the midst of our suffering as he died on the cross, us in the midst of God's suffering as we ached deep inside us.

I wept for them all: Cairo, Dave, the jar. I wept for God in his crucifixion. And as I took the time to feel the pain, a most surprising thing happened. I was overwhelmed by wonder and thankfulness. I felt a sense of ultimate well-being gently seeping through from within, deeper than the pain, deeper than the wrongness. Permeating into my innermost aching there was a fluid, irrepressible peace. It was a sense that at the end of the day, no matter how awful it had been, all would be well. It was a gut knowledge that the evil and the wrongness did not have the last word, just as Jesus was resurrected rather than left on the cross. From my tenderness there was the faith that, in ways ranging from the ordinary to the mysterious, all would be transformed, just as Jesus, who met the agony head on in his death, was transformed into an aliveness he had not known on earth. In Jesus, God displayed that all pain, no matter how deep and brutal, could be recreated into life, more whole, vibrant and complete than if the pain had never occurred in the first place.

So that was why God did not annihilate suffering from this earth. That was why he did not scrap human beings and say, 'Well, that little universe was a bit of a dead loss. Let's scrub it and start all over again.' He had something better up his sleeve. He acted within the problems we already had. He used, as his raw material, pain. He took what was broken, what was hurting, what was wrong, and transformed it into something beautiful, lovely and good. Life out of death, good out of bad, was the meaning of redemption.

And I realized as I prayed by the river that night that my pain was being transformed and redeemed. The sense of human fragility and vulnerability engendered by the past few months no longer trapped me in fear. It liberated me. The knowledge that I could die at any moment enabled me to live richly in the present. It freed me into a grateful acceptance of what each day brings so I could live deeply and yet lightly. Looking death squarely in the face, I was less afraid of swinging in the Big Dipper, walking down dark streets and flying in aeroplanes. I was going to die anyway. I could say 'yes' to the now.

God redeems – I grasped it in my guts. And that was what made it possible for me to confront the pain I encountered then and future pains to come. It gave me courage to stay with it. I could see how uncreative it was to cut myself off from all that I found frightening and strange within. Every time I ate compulsively, wrapping a blanket around myself, I was running away not only from the cross but also from the resurrection. I was missing out on the transformation of what I and the world had suffered. I did not want to do that.

That was what I had done for four years. I had been

refusing the responsibility of being my own person. I had been shielding myself from the appalling suffering in the world. I had been sheltering from the pain of my parents' divorce and refusing to enter into the aches of other people. I had been hiding from death. Learning how to pray and to eat was to feel not only the agony of gone-wrongness but the even deeper joy of recreatedness.

In some ways my compulsive eating years were a waste. What a shame to spend four years afraid of swimming, walking, parties, cuddling and living; what a waste to be so unhappy during my late teens and early twenties – how stupid to have believed such lies. But now that I have had the courage to face those years head on and heart on, I do not look on them with regret. I believe nothing has gone to waste; it has all been transformed. I am glad my compulsive eating years are behind me, but I am even more glad they have happened. Now I can eat normally, I am not on a par with those who have never had the struggle that I have had to get there. For there is something even better than never having had an eating disorder, and that is having an eating disorder redeemed. Now that I have emerged from the compulsive eater's tunnel and a chocolate bar and I can share a room together, now that I no longer respond to every situation by walking into the larder, I can see that my disorder has saved me.

Who would I have been if I had never been a compulsive eater? The experience is now so much a part of me that any answer can only be speculative, but I do not think I would have been the kind of person I like to know. I fancied I was clever and competent. I did not succeed in everything but I succeeded in all that I cared about. I had no comprehension of why people became alcoholics, beat up their wives, stayed in bed until one o'clock or stole pocket handkerchiefs from the supermarket. I had a hard confidence that I could get out of life whatever I wanted. I imagined I was in control and that I coped.

My compulsion has given me a grateful softness. It is the softness of knowing deep down that I am who I am because of those who have loved me. It was the love of Anne, of Renee, of

Liz, of Pamela, of Steve, of Jane, and of countless others as well as God that healed me. It was their steady acceptance, their sure faith in me that freed me into an acceptance and a faith in myself . Who deserves to be loved like that? No one and everyone – humanity in general and each person in particular. Their love has released in me a rock-bottom 'Thank you'.

Opening my heart to receive the love which has been poured in means holding it open so that that love might flow out. I no longer listen to a drug addict with a baffled incomprehension, but in the understanding that he and I stand in the same place before God. I am better able to see myself and others in terms of our vulnerable, tender insides rather than our 'failing', blundering outsides. My compulsion has evoked in me the desire to touch people and to love them as I have been loved.

My eating disorder showed me a new face of God. It pointed me to the one intricately bound up in us and yet totally beyond us. It has put me in touch with parts of myself that were deeper than I had known before, making me more gutsy in my prayer and more gentle in my action.

I had fought against my eating disorder. I had to learn to embrace it. In embracing my weakness I was rescued from what I had perceived as my strengths. How unsurprising! I was saved by my weakness. Wasn't that what my faith should have led me to believe would happen all the way along? Wasn't Jesus a wandering man who focused his ministry on the ordinary, the poor, and the funny man stuck up a tree?

O God, you turn our values on their heads. You turn us upside down with the more-wonderful-than-we-dared-hope-for sense of your kingdom. Here is each day I have eaten compulsively, every glance in a shop window through which I have hated my body. Here is each missed opportunity because I thought myself fat. Here are Greg the homeless, Nora dying of cancer, Ian the gambler, Mary the bereaved. Here are the poor and wounded parts of ourselves and of our world.

There is in God, some say
    a deep but dazzling darkness . . .

Henry Vaughan, Night

Methinks there is in God
    a well of laughter very deep . . .

Jim Cotter, Prayer at Night
(Cairns Publications)

Recipe

Marmite, cream cheese and lettuce sandwich

Ingredients:

A fresh, round granary loaf – four slices
A large pot of Marmite – one knife-load
A polystyrene carton of cream cheese – several knife-loads
An Iceberg lettuce – a handful

Method:

1. Take the bread from the basket.
2. Hold it in your hands, feel its weight, squeeze it.
3. Slice it, listening to the sound of the knife through the crust.
4. Feel the texture of the grains with your fingers.
5. Open the jar of Marmite.
6. Smell it, remember your childhood.
7. Observe the gluey consistency of the spread as you scoop it on to the knife.
8. Spread it on half the slices of bread. Look at the difference in its colour when it is thick and when it is thin.
9. Enjoy the perfect whiteness of the cream cheese in the white carton.
10. Stick your finger in if it would help you enjoy its texture.
11. Using a knife, spread the cheese on top of the Marmite and look at the contrast between the brown and the white.

12. Break open the lettuce and notice how cold it feels.
13. Do not wash it, tear a handful from the clean heart.
14. Put it on the slices of bread covered in Marmite and cream cheese.
15. Put the dry slices of bread on top of the lettuce and press down, enjoying the spongey feel.
16. Go and sit down.
17. Eat it, as much as you want.